I0568316

ESCAPE FROM MARIUPOL

A Survivor's True Story

ADORIANA MARIK

As Told To Award-Winning Author

ANNE K. HOWARD

WILDBLUE
PRESS

WildBluePress.com

ESCAPE FROM MARIUPOL published by:
WILDBLUE PRESS
P.O. Box 102440
Denver, Colorado 80250

Publisher Disclaimers: Any opinions, statements of fact or fiction, descriptions, dialogue, and citations found in this book were provided by the author and are solely those of the author. The publisher makes no claim as to their veracity or accuracy and assumes no liability for the content. Names of individuals have been changed to protect their privacy.

Copyright 2022 by Anne K. Howard

All rights reserved. No part of this book may be reproduced in any form or by any means without the prior written consent of the Publisher, excepting brief quotes used in reviews.

WILDBLUE PRESS is registered at the U.S. Patent and Trademark Offices.

ISBN 978-1-957288-84-0 Hardcover
ISBN 978-1-957288-85-7 Trade Paperback
ISBN 978-1-957288-99-4 eBook

Cover design © 2022 WildBlue Press. All rights reserved.
Interior Formatting and Book Cover Design by Elijah Toten
www.totencreative.com

ESCAPE FROM MARIUPOL

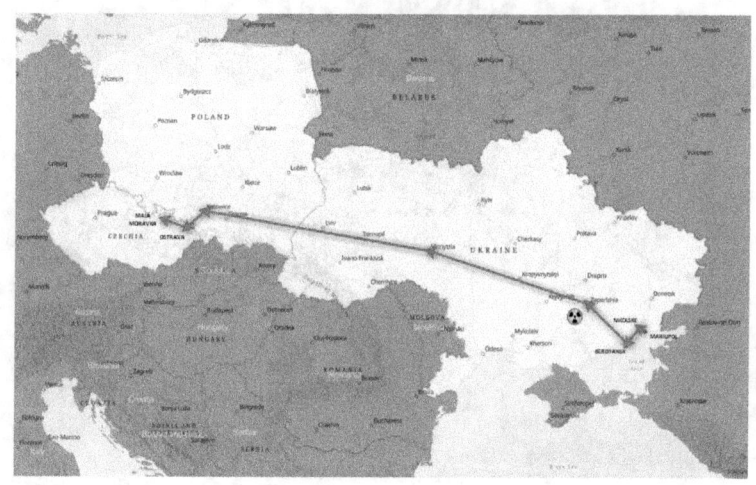

Adoriana's Escape Route

Introduction

I first became acquainted with the Ukrainian author of this book, Adoriana Marik, over twenty years ago. I was searching online for a Ukrainian nanny to move to America and take care of my two young children while I built a busy law practice. I am part Polish, and I have always been fascinated with Eastern Europe—the rich, cultural history, the many lyrical languages, and the sumptuous food.

I contacted a young woman named Inna Marik, a nineteen-year-old who was eager to leave Mariupol, Ukraine, and move to the United States. Unfortunately, it was too difficult for Inna to obtain a work visa, so I ended up hiring a Polish nanny. Inna and I remained in close touch over the years, with her younger sister, Adoriana, sometimes sending me artwork and hand-drawn cards she created.

Inna eventually moved to the US and married an American. When Russia invaded Ukraine in the early morning hours of February 24, 2022, I contacted Inna to see if Adoriana was still in Mariupol. The horrific images of Russia's merciless attack on the seaport city sent chills up my spine. Was Adoriana trapped inside one of those countless bombed-out apartment buildings? God forbid she was one of the many civilian corpses the drone imagery revealed to the world.

Inna told me she did not know where Adoriana was or if she had fled the carnage in Mariupol. She could not connect to Adoriana's cell phone, and she feared for her younger sister's life. It turns out, Adoriana was hiding with her beloved husky, Yola, in a basement shelter beneath a high-rise building in the center of Mariupol. Over two hundred civilians hid in that shelter, enduring horrendous conditions. It was the middle of winter and there was no heat underground, very little food or water, and no essential medicines. Adoriana was surrounded by suffering and death. She literally slept beside human corpses.

After five weeks of hell, she emerged to the street above to see a city she no longer recognized: Russia had razed Mariupol to the ground. The story of how Adoriana escaped Mariupol illustrates one woman's indomitable spirit and will to survive.

I contacted Adoriana by email in April 2022. She was living in a refugee hostel in the Czech Republic with Yola still by her side. She told me about her experiences living underground and escaping through Russian-occupied territory in eastern Ukraine. I have represented many individuals suffering from PTSD in my law practice over the years. Some of them are war vets. Nevertheless, I have never met someone who experienced the same level of relentless, life-threatening trauma as Adoriana experienced in the early months of Russia's invasion. Her harrowing story begged to be written and shared.

Adoriana agreed to join me in a collaborative effort and write the book you are about to read. In the following months, she sent me numerous emails, written in Russian, the second language of many Ukrainians, in which she provided a detailed account of her journey. I translated her words into English and crafted her story, providing footnotes when required. In this age of disinformation, I've attempted to reference a diverse group of sources rather than drawing from a single news outlet. I also tried to be as true to Adoriana's voice as possible. This story is one hundred percent fact-based, with names and very minor details changed to protect the identities of the people involved.

Adoriana once said that I was "psychology in a bottle." Sharing her trauma with me was part of her healing process. I am not a psychologist or a jinni, however. I simply provided her with a safe place to vent her emotions, which I suppose is what any good friend would do.

As I write this introduction, Russia's war of attrition is not going as Russia's president, Vladimir Putin, had planned. With the help of NATO support, Ukraine is making significant gains and Ukrainian soldiers are more determined than ever to defend their homeland. In contrast, Russia's soldiers are losing morale and Russian citizens are starting to question the legitimacy of Putin's mismanaged "military operation." In turn, Putin continues to make veiled threats of tactical nuclear retaliation and recently announced the mobilization of three hundred thousand additional reservists with military backgrounds to fight in Ukraine.

At a time when American democracy is under threat, along with many democracies throughout the world, the Ukrainian people—warriors and civilians alike—are showing the world what it means to fight for freedom: not just for themselves but for future generations. May God bless and protect every democracy in existence, and may God bless and protect Ukraine.

Anne K. Howard
September 22, 2022

What is the end of war for us? We used to say peace—now we say victory.
— **President Volodymyr Zelensky,
Ukraine Independence Day, August 24, 2022**

Preface

I'm trapped inside a catacomb. The vaults above take a direct hit from Russian projectiles and erupt into flames. Clouds of ink-black smoke snake through the underground corridors. I choke for breath as Russian soldiers pour inside, pointing assault rifles at civilians and indiscriminately shooting, the seamless line of bullets crackling in quick succession.

BRRRRRRRRRRRRRRRRRRTTTTTTTTTTTTTT!
BRRRRRRRRRRRRRRRRTTTTTTTTTTTTTTTT!

A Russian soldier chases after me. I race up the stairway and flee into the street. Outside, the air is cold, yet fire is everywhere. A murder of crows perches above the skeletal framework of tall-standing megaliths. Russian soldiers approach from behind. They pull out plastic water guns and shoot me in the back. *Splash!*

"You got me!" I shout.

I wake up laughing crazed, maniacal laughter. *That was one hell of a nightmare.* Eyes still shut, I go about mentally preparing for my day. I have only two days left of vacation, so I had better hurry up and get to work on renovating the bathroom. After that, I'll take Yola for a walk in City Theater Square.

I open my eyes. Reality intervenes. I'm not in the bedroom of my apartment in Mariupol. I lay inside the attic of a refugee hostel in the Czech Republic. *It wasn't a dream,* I realize dismally. *The nightmare was real.*

My name is Adoriana Marik. I'm a thirty-two-year-old tattoo artist and merchandiser who lived in the once beautiful port city of Mariupol, Ukraine. The life I enjoyed in Mariupol seems like a far-off dream to me now. It was by no means a perfect existence, but I was safe and free. I had friends, family, and my beloved dog, a husky named Yola. In those simple things, I saw a full-fledged and peaceful life that no one could take away from me. Overnight, my world was permanently and tragically altered by the Russian invasion. Today, I am a refugee.

This is my story. I do not speak for all Ukrainian refugees, nor do I pretend to be a scholar on the facts surrounding Russia's brutal invasion of Ukraine. I am simply one woman with a story to share with those who are willing to listen.

Chapter One

I was born in June 1990. At the time, my parents and two elder siblings lived in an unassuming three-bedroom apartment in a modernized section of Mariupol. A balcony overlooked a road where pedestrians bustled past, and a loggia hovered above a grassy courtyard.

Most of the buildings in the twenty-third micro-district had nine stories, with fourteen-storied buildings located a few blocks away. In those days, the visual appeal of Mariupol was far less alluring than what it would become in subsequent decades. The brutalist architecture was ugly and plain. Buildings were slabs of concrete with raw textures, designed for utilitarian purposes. There were few parks where trees and flowers could grow, and even fewer foreign restaurants.

The palatial Drama Theater located in Teatral'na Square was an exception to this uncultivated and coarse character. With its brick-red roof, towering white walls, beveled columns, and rudimentary arches, the colossal structure evoked the Mediterranean Sea and Roman times. Every Christmas season, a giant, fresh-cut evergreen tree, laced with ornamental bulbs and glowing lights, was placed outside the theater.

I recall walking past the Drama Theater as a small child. My mother exclaimed, "*Moya vyshen'ka*, look at the beautiful tree!" *Moya vyshen'ka*—meaning "my little cherry"—was her affectionate pet name for me. It was a uniquely Ukrainian endearment; cherries are our national fruit and constitute the main ingredient of many of our recipes, including the traditional Ukrainian varenyky, a crescent-shaped dough similar to ravioli, stuffed with sweet, syrupy cherries, or other items like potato, cabbage, or salo (pork meat). Cherry varenyky are best complemented by sour cream. If varenyky are not your style, you can always try traditional cherry *babka* ("cake").

In 1990, the first competitive elections to the Ukrainian parliament resulted in the establishment of parliamentary opposition and declaration of the sovereignty of the republic still within the USSR.[1] My parents later told me about how different Ukrainian life had been under Soviet control. Everyone had a job, they said, and everyone was busy. Ukrainian citizens lived modestly but their essential needs were met. It sounded to me like there was a herd mindset in which no one stood out or questioned the commands of Soviet leadership.

In comparison, the Ukrainian democratic government that followed the fall of the Soviet Union in 1991 brought with it a daunting host of new demands. It was difficult for many Ukrainians to make the transition from being given instructions from autocratic leaders on how to live their day-to-day lives to suddenly needing to work more with their brains and not their hands. Under the new democratic rule, Ukrainians were instantly allowed the freedom to choose for themselves how they wished to live and seek self-expression. It was as though everyone was collectively pushed off a pier and forced to sink or swim.

Most Ukrainians learned to swim, taking great satisfaction in knowing they could question their leaders and vote for better ones if they were not happy with the direction the country was moving in. As we bathed in the

---

1. Plokhy, Serhi. *The Gates of Europe: A History of Ukraine*. New York: Basic Books. 2021. p. 377.

waters of democracy, we realized that everything depends on the individual and their choices. Why purchase Soviet bread buns for three kopecks when you can open a bakery and make your own?

That is not to say that the waters of democracy equated with smooth sailing. There were many political storms—some of them were Category 5 hurricanes. In 2004, when I was thirteen years old, the Democratic Orange Revolution commenced. Ukrainians protested the government's corruption and Russian interference in our electoral process. The Orange Revolution resulted in the installation of a pro-reform and pro-Western government led by President Viktor Yushchenko.[2]

Still, Ukrainians were not one hundred percent united in the spirit of democracy. People squabbled amongst themselves without attempting to look at issues from a global perspective. I remember one girl at school criticizing me for wearing an orange sweater, claiming it represented my support for the Orange Revolution. It was an absurd accusation. I was simply wearing an orange sweater. On that day, I learned an important lesson: Rats live amongst us. Certain minds are not healthy. They seek to exchange our hard-won freedoms and nostalgically revert to a Soviet-controlled past.

My early childhood was defined by loneliness and boredom. My father worked long hours to provide for our family, and my sister and brother were teenagers, already absorbed in their activities. I spent many hours alone in the apartment as my mother made the two-hour journey to care for her elderly parents in an outlying village.

When I returned from school each day, I roamed the streets in search of a stray dog I had named Lassie. A cross between a German shepherd and a mongrel, Lassie was a titanic black dog who quickly attached herself to me.

---

2. Plokhy. *The Gates of Europe*. p. 377.

Everyone told me to stay away from her, but I refused. I walked everywhere with Lassie and even purchased a collar for her using my pocket money.

I was not allowed to bring Lassie home, so I took food from our apartment and brought it to her in the street. Once, as Lassie was eating some meat and bread crusts I had placed on the pavement, another dog, belonging to a local woman, attacked. The dog was a fighting breed. He ferociously dove at Lassie's neck, tearing into it with his teeth.

I attempted to separate the dogs, but the woman who owned the other dog grabbed me and would not let me intervene. A man approached. He lifted a large brick from the ground and threw it at the head of the attacking dog. Only then did the dog remove his teeth from Lassie's neck. The owner hooked her dog on a leash and marched off.

Lassie writhed on the ground in pain. I knelt beside her and stroked her blood-streaked pelt. My parents emerged from the apartment building and took me home, leaving Lassie wounded and alone in the street. I searched the following day and found her surrounded by a crowd of boys in the yard where we played. They were laughing and throwing stones at her. She scurried away, her tail locked between her legs, and went to die under the porch of a house. The heartless boys pursued her and continued to throw stones.

In a fit of rage, I grabbed a large tree branch and drove away the savage thugs, knocking out the tooth of one of them in the process. I then crawled beneath the porch and treated Lassie's wounds, which were already infested with maggots.

When my parents found out about the incident, they were shocked. "You cannot walk that dog anymore!" they ordered.

Defiant, I told them I would not return home if they forbade me to walk Lassie. To my surprise, they relented. After that, I did not have many friends in the neighborhood.

I was fine with that so long as I had Lassie at my side. Her wounds gradually healed, although one of her torn ears was permanently damaged and sagged at an awkward angle, giving her a funny look.

The boy whose tooth I knocked out threatened to poison Lassie when I was not around. One day, animal control arrived. Lassie was taken to the animal shelter and euthanized for allegedly biting one of the boys. I wept as I discovered her collar in the street. I held on to it as a keepsake, storing it in the little drawer of my night table.

Chapter Two

My parents moved to the village when I was in elementary school. My mother's parents had recently passed away. She missed them and preferred living in the house they had left for her, where she'd grown up, surrounded by sentimental memories of earlier times. I couldn't join them. There was no school in the village, no hospital, no police.

And so, I stayed behind in the apartment in Mariupol with my brother and sister, who were now in their twenties and capable of looking after me. My parents visited often, and family gatherings were always friendly and warm. As the years passed, my mother would visit and share stories about problems they were having in the village, how alcoholic and drug-addicted villagers would threaten my parents in their yards. I told them, again and again, to return to the city where it was safe, but they refused to leave. Looking back on it now, perhaps it was good they did not return to Mariupol.

I celebrated my eighteenth birthday in June 2008 by treating my friend Katya to brunch at The Garden Café. The high-end restaurant was a one-minute walk from the beach. Wide balconies on the second floor offered a stunning view of the Sea of Azov. On the main floor, a wedding reception was taking place. The bride glowed with happiness. For Katya and me, she embodied the hopeful future that lay ahead of us.

The workers at The Garden Café were friendly and efficient. In my humble opinion, there is no better service sector than in Ukraine. I have traveled around Europe and I have never encountered the same uniformly high level of hospitality. This also applies to our beauty industry. Many can confirm that a large percentage of Ukrainians simply have golden hands.

Katya and I spent the remainder of the afternoon strolling the City Garden, a historic park featuring monuments to the soldiers who died in the Civil War and the Great Patriotic War. The sprawling plaza was a terrific place for two restless teenagers to cut loose and have a little fun. There were amusement park rides, including a Ferris wheel, a shooting gallery, playgrounds, and summer cinemas, to name a few attractions. A warm breeze blew off the sea, sprinkling our hair with saltwater droplets. White and yellow tulips colored the grassy grounds. European roller birds and tawny pipits flitted happily through the swaying branches of pines and beech. How wonderful it was to be eighteen and live in Mariupol!

As the sun lowered over the waters of the Azov Sea, Katya and I returned to her family's apartment, where her mother prepared uzvar for us, a non-alcoholic drink made from fruits and grains. Katya's sister joined us as we discussed light topics: the weather, our summer plans, new music we were listening to—anything *except* politics.

That said, escalating tensions between Ukraine and Russia were an ongoing concern for all Ukrainians. From 2008 to 2009, Ukraine proclaimed its intent to join the European Union and applied for NATO membership. In response, Russia began a trade war with Ukraine in 2013. The trade war forced the government of Viktor Yanukovych to back out of signing an association agreement with the EU. Yanukovych's decision sparked mass protests that became known as the Euromaidan, leading to the Revolution of Dignity in 2014. The protests in the streets of our nation's capital, Kiev, turned violent. Amidst the civil unrest, the Ukrainian parliament removed President Yanukovych from office while Russia launched a hybrid war against Ukraine.[3]

In 2014, Russia illegally annexed the Crimean Peninsula, which is situated along the northern coast of the Black Sea in eastern Ukraine. The peninsula's population of 2.4 million is mostly composed of ethnic Russians, with an appreciable amount of Ukrainian and Crimean Tatar minorities, and a smattering of other ethnicities.[4] Compared to the seismic conflict that would one day devastate Mariupol, the hybrid war had a minimal impact on the residents of Mariupol, although there were several small terrorist attacks in remote areas of the city.

When the left bank district of Mariupol was shelled in 2014, I left for Odesa, a port city along the Black Sea in southern Ukraine, and lived there for a few months until the fighting died down. I was twenty-two years old and still clung to the hope that a bloodthirsty Putin was satiated by his small-scale victory and would leave the rest of Ukraine alone.

Nevertheless, the presence of Russian troops and supplies in the Donbas region, which comprised about 4.4 percent of the Ukrainian population, was an ominous reminder of Russia's formidable military threat. It marked the most critical crisis in East-West relations since the end of the Cold War.[5] Not a day went by when I did not worry about the possibility of more Russian attacks. Despite that fear, I went on with my life, finding restorative escape in the worlds of art and music.

My love for painting and drawing was passed on to me by my mother, who once worked as an artist in the cinema. Mama painted huge posters when there was no printing in

---

3. Plokhy. *The Gates of Europe*. p. 377

4. Plokhy. *The Gates of Europe*. p. 377.

5. Ibid.

this format. Seeing her exquisite placards motivated me to take a paintbrush in my hand earlier than a spoon.

The drawing, the art, was never about competing with anyone else—it was about the exploration of beauty. I could spend hours looking at a leaf on a tree, tracing its intricate patterns with my eyes, or focus on an elegant advertisement. Creating art is a form of meditation. It doesn't matter what form it takes: whether on canvas, paper, wall, clothing, or human skin. Beauty has the power to heal, enlighten, and magically transport us to higher realms.

My close friend, Vanko, introduced me to the art of drawing tattoos; he asked me to sketch something special for him. Vanko handed the sketch to a tattoo artist to etch on his arm. Word spread in the military service building where he worked. Soon, men from the military knocked on my door, requesting custom-designed tattoos. I enrolled in courses at a reputable tattoo studio with a network of salons throughout Europe. I also sold my paintings at a gallery in a local shopping center. Seeing others enjoy my works brought tremendous pleasure and purpose to my life.

But let's not forget the music! In my twenties, I attended many concerts in Kiev featuring bands like Limp Bizkit, a rap-rock band from Jacksonville, Florida. The nu-metal sonic experimentation of Limp Bizkit is not for everyone. My older sister hated the music. We sometimes fought when I cranked up the volume at home in my teen years. The aggressively intense rhythms connected with an unknown yearning inside of me. Despite the amount of swearing in the lyrics, the concert hall where Limp Bizkit performed possessed an indescribably powerful atmosphere. You could almost touch the energy as it rose above the throngs of cheering fans. Other concert favorites included bands like Korn, P.O.D., The Deftones, and many others.

My days of attending concerts abruptly ended when the pandemic began in early 2020. At the start of 2022, Ukrainians, like most of the world's population, had lockdown fatigue. We all wore face masks in public, except for inside restaurants and bars. Months earlier, I had helped to take care of Vanko, who was extremely sick with COVID. Vanko's temperature hovered at 40°C (104°F), and nothing took the temperature down. His plight reminded me of a scene in the original *Jacob's Ladder*, a classic horror film in which the main character, played by Tim Robbins, is plunged into a tub of ice to cool the fever before it affects his brain.

Vanko's parents and I feared we would lose him forever. We could not call an ambulance because they would not come for COVID patients. We were discouraged from driving him to the hospital as we were told the hospitals were all overcrowded. Adding to our sense of helplessness was the fact that Vanko had allergic reactions to a large number of antibiotics. Thankfully, we had a friend who was a doctor who would visit and offer instruction. I learned to give Vanko the injections he needed, including Augmentin. Strangely, neither Vanko's parents nor I were infected with COVID at that time, even though we did not wear masks at home. Perhaps we did catch COVID and were asymptomatic, who knows.

The tattoo parlor where I worked forced its staff to get vaccinated or lose their jobs. The only vaccine readily available then was AstraZeneca, likely because it's cheaper than other vaccines and easier to distribute due to not needing to be frozen while in storage; AstraZeneca's vaccine can remain refrigerated for up to six months. That's the good news.

The bad news is the AstraZeneca shot made me extremely ill for four days with symptoms that mirrored a nasty case of COVID: a temperature of almost 40°C, severe muscle pains rendering me immobile, splitting headaches, and nausea. I cursed the day I went for that vaccine. By the time the second shot came due, the Pfizer vaccine was available. I received the Pfizer shot and experienced only mild side effects: a sore arm and a headache. Compared to what I was to suffer in the months ahead, the pain now seems trivial.

Chapter Three

In the winter of 2022, I had the apartment I'd grown up in all to myself. I knew how lucky I was to live there rent-free, although the modest space still belonged to my parents in every respect. I could not make any changes or repairs without first gaining their permission.

My days were jam-packed with work-related obligations. I woke up early and returned home late, sometimes working on weekends as well. My friends would chastise me, "Adoriana, you will finish yourself off with such a life! You need to take a vacation!"

Time off would have been nice, but I could not afford the luxury of traveling to another country. I needed to save up every hryvnia I earned in hopes of getting a job in another country—one not constantly threatened by impending war. In the meantime, I planned to take a staycation at the end of February 2022. Although I usually took time off in the summer, I had a hunch I would need to rest up for what lay ahead. I also had a lot of projects I wanted to complete, and making cosmetic repairs to my bathroom was at the top of the list.

Unfortunately, Ukrainians don't have the best attitude about dogs. In Mariupol, there were no designated parks or walkways for dogs and their owners, and few people took responsibility for strays. After several parts of the city were restored or rebuilt, iron boxes containing plastic bags were placed beneath lampposts to encourage people to clean up after their dogs. Within days, all of the boxes were stolen. There were also a lot of syringes lying on the pavement in dangerous neighborhoods, making it risky for dogs. With this in mind, I took Yola for long walks by the seaside on the weekends. Sometimes we also jogged along the Kal'mius River, where the coal chimneys of the Azovstal Steel Plant loomed against the canvas of a smokey winter sky.

The behemoth steel plant sprawled across 4.2 square miles, with warehouses and coal factories covering a vast labyrinth of underground tunnels. The Kal'mius River runs along one side of the plant, and the Sea of Azov borders the other side. I often felt resentment as I jogged past the plant. True, it helped our local economy by employing thirty thousand Ukrainians in its factories and warehouses. Nevertheless, the oligarch who owned the plant—Renat Akhmetov, one of the wealthiest men in Ukraine—refused to install purification filters, despite earning billions of dollars in profits.

For decades, residents breathed in harmful emissions strong enough to create a thick smog that never left the city. If you cleaned your house in the evening, the furniture would be coated with a thin veil of dust and shiny metal grains by morning. If you rubbed your finger across a windowsill, your fingertip would turn black. Children were covered in dust and metal grains as they walked to school and played in the streets. The ecological disaster was something the residents were forced to grudgingly accept.

Many outsiders were baffled by the apparent complacency of Ukrainians in the weeks preceding Russia's invasion. News outlets showed footage of citizens going about their daily activities, seemingly without a care in the world. Even our president, Volodymyr Zelensky, presented as calm and relatively unalarmed when United States intelligence indicated about one hundred and fifty thousand Russian troops had amassed at our borders. I can assure you that the air in Ukraine was thick with rising tension. Most residents were deeply stressed. Understandably, President Zelensky was intent on preventing mass panic.

I felt a distinct, almost otherworldly sense of foreboding in the months leading up to the invasion. Like the second witch in *Macbeth*, I intuited that "something wicked this way" was coming. My disquiet prompted me to organize all of my legal documents, including my passport and Yola's vaccination records, and store them in a safe location in my apartment. I added a few family photos to the stash, including pictures of my paternal relatives who lived in Russia.

Food prices rose incommensurate with salaries. The requirements at my workplace increased, but my salary remained the same. Three days before the war began, I finally took the vacation my friends had been begging me to take. I wanted to figure out what my next step would be. Should I find another job in Ukraine? Move away? Where would I go, and how would I come up with the money to get there, let alone live there?

I carried these worries with me as I walked with Yola to our favorite café, Mr. Bean and Bowler Hat, on my first day of vacation. Named after the quirky title character of the popular British sitcom, the quaint establishment was only a few steps away from the gorgeously renovated City Theater Square. In warmer weather, an outdoor stage was assembled for various events and concerts, and the city's most important Christmas tree still glowed outside the Drama Theater every Yuletide.

The Drama Theater was located in a historic part of Mariupol. The neighborhood's largely ethnic Greek population resulted from when the Greeks helped the Russian Empire, under the rule of Catherine the Great, against the Turks. Many of the homes and structures were built in the 1800s. Most feature small balconies facing the street from which neighbors would greet each other as pedestrians pass below. A museum dedicated to Mariupol's maritime history as a major port stood down the block.

Restaurants featuring Italian and Georgian cuisine now offered Ukrainians a wider culinary menu to enjoy. Whereas our taste buds were familiar with relatively bland staple foods like borscht, a beet soup made with beef, cabbage, and root vegetables, the introduction of Italian spinach ricotta and zesty chicken parmesan was a welcome change. The cheesy comfort food and spicy yogurt-based dishes served at the Georgian bistros were also scrumptious. I rarely drink alcohol, but I am told that Georgian Qvevri wines, which are fermented in clay vessels and buried underground, are delicious.

Since President Zelensky came to power with an impressive seventy-three percent of the Ukrainian vote in 2019, the squares and streets in the old section of the city were repaired and restored. Magnificent buildings and manicured parks seemed to sprout up from the ground overnight. What remained unchanged were the flocks of pigeons roaming the sidewalks, taking flight above the batches of lively teenagers riding skateboards and bicycles.

Thanks to Zelensky's initiatives, the western section of Mariupol assumed a European flavor and life was always in full swing. In the daylight hours, people walked under a graceful stone arch and passed the time sitting on benches and conversing as the cool fog of evening approached. At night, the crowded squares awakened with the sound of live music encircling colorfully lit fountains. In the winter, we skated at the ice rink and purchased hot chocolates, hamburgers, and pastries from the many food carts and fast-food franchises nearby.

Mr. Bean was one of the few eateries in Mariupol where dogs were allowed inside. Of course, Yola loved going to Mr. Bean and Bowler Hat. She would nestle beneath my legs and rest her head on my feet, her wet black nose inhaling the sweet and savory scents of rich cheesecake, smoked salmon, and eggs Benedict. That day, I chatted over coffee with my friends for hours, finding much-needed solace in their company. We were all in this together, for better or for worse.

The café's atmosphere was a curative balm to our fragile nerves. Like Mr. Bean, the open room was warm and unapologetically offbeat. In one corner, a pseudo-Victorian sofa and matching wingback chairs upholstered in mustard-colored faux leather welcomed patrons to relax. Industrial lights hung from above. Lush ferns soaked up the heatless winter sunlight pouring in through tall-standing windows. Little did my friends and I know that it would be the last time we would enjoy the food and hip character of our esteemed Mr. Bean.

I recently searched for the café on social media. Sadly, it was bombed during the invasion, as were the vast majority of the buildings in Mariupol. My heart sank as I looked at the heap of bricks and debris. This is the harsh reality of any war, but especially Putin's war. Quiet pleasures and natural beauty are destroyed. Architecturally stunning museums, parks, libraries, and restaurants are wiped off the map, replaced by bullet casings, corpses, and ash.

Tears pricked my eyes as I came across the last remaining photos of Mr. Bean and Bowler Hat on Facebook. The staff posed before a Christmas tree on December 30, 2021, waving sparklers in the air. Their faces beamed with happiness. Ironically, on the chalkboard behind them, these words were written in English:

New Year is Coming! Spend last days with Mr. Bean!

The final photo on the Mr. Bean and Bowler Hat Facebook page was posted on February 21, three days before the war began. It depicts a masked waitress stretching her arm upward in triumph, eyes smiling before the camera, as a co-worker watches on. The post is captioned: *Waiting for Spring! #peoplefooddrink*. The photo reflects the hope the residents of our city were determined to hold on to as copious Russian tanks loomed in the shadows.

Chapter Four

"Double, double toil and trouble; fire
burn and cauldron bubble."
— *The Tragedy of Macbeth,* Act 4, Scene 1

I went to bed on the evening of February 23, 2022, sedated by the tapping of freezing rain against the windowpanes and the eerie silence that the city curfew brought to the streets below. At about 4 a.m., after a month of rattling his saber, President Vladimir Putin made good on his threat to attack his peaceful neighbor. I awoke to the sound of several powerful explosions. My friend, Luda, immediately phoned me.

"Did you hear the explosions?" she asked frantically. "Has the war begun? What to do?"

I told Luda I would go to her and, together, we would decide what to do next. I had to act quickly. I was in flight-or-fight mode, like an animal in the forest running away from a predator. In the space of a few seconds, I leashed Yola and threw my documents and her dog food into my backpack. I stumbled out of the apartment building, pure terror racing through my mind. My skin was covered in goosebumps as I experienced a nauseating feeling of inevitability. *Brace yourself,* I thought, *do whatever you can to survive.*

In the dimly lit streets, panic-stricken drivers violated the rules instructing residents to stay within city limits. In the distance, a traffic jam comprising hundreds of cars stretched for several kilometers. It was like a scene from an apocalyptic movie. As I tore down the sidewalk in the direction of Luda's apartment, cars chaotically whizzed past at high speeds, failing to brake for stop signs and red lights. Who cared about abiding by the rules when the sky was on fire?

The outside temperature was 3°C but the powerful wind that blew in from the sea made the cold air more palpable. I squinted through the smog that perpetually filled our streets, the result of emissions from several metallurgical plants. The smell of oxidized metal was everywhere, but there was nothing new about that.

Luda and her husband Ivan lived ten minutes away. I made it to their apartment in record time and I recounted what was happening outside. "I must leave the city," I said.

"We won't go with you," Luda said. "Ivan's father is sick. He doesn't walk. We have a cat and a dog. Where would we go?"

Ivan joined in: "I think no one will bomb civilians. We have the infrastructure here—factories, a massive steel plant. Why would Russia want to destroy the city?"

"We need to calm down," Luda intervened. "Maybe they can agree on peace…."

Even then, I did not hold out much hope for peace. While Putin didn't have a strong record for reasonable negotiations, he was known to bullishly seize lands that did not belong to him. As for Mariupol's infrastructure and civilians, Putin couldn't have cared less. He wanted the land, the rivers, and the sea, and he was willing to carry out savage crimes against humanity to achieve his goal. I later learned that the initial artillery bombardment injured twenty-six people. The following day, Russian forces advanced from Donetsk People's Republic (DPR) territory in the east towards Mariupol.

In the days that followed, I searched for a way to get out of the city. I had no car, and there were no tickets for the bus. With great difficulty, I managed to find a train ticket to Ivano-Frankivsk, but the day the train was scheduled to arrive, the Russians blew up a branch of the railway tracks in Volnovakha, and all the routes out of Mariupol were cut off.

I was trapped. I stayed with Luda and Ivan inside the windowless vestibule in the center of their apartment building. Explosions sounded in the streets below. The air raid sirens were almost useless. They were practically inaudible, especially in buildings with soundproofed windows. They were also unreliable, often sounding after an explosion occurred rather than before. We learned to rely on notifications texted to our phones.

A strict 5 p.m. evening curfew was enforced. I still believed the evacuation of civilians was imminent, and that outside groups like the Red Cross would come to rescue us. I continued to be proactive in my quest to escape. I used my phone to reach out to many online volunteer groups for assistance. No one responded to my desperate pleas.

Even if I could get out of the city, I had no idea where I would settle. My childhood friend, Katya, was now living in Poland. She once told me it was very hard to find employment and afford an apartment. I considered moving to Germany or Italy or perhaps the Czech Republic. However, at that early stage in the crisis, such deliberations rested in the back recesses of my mind. My greatest objective was to stay alive.

I considered running to the Drama Theater, which was located in the heart of the city, and seeking shelter with other civilians. The theater was one of the larger shelters. I associated the building with safety. Huge and sturdy, it provided physical protection that Luda and Ivan's vestibule did not. Ukrainians had painted the word "CHILDREN" in giant letters on the grounds surrounding the theater to ward off aerial attacks. In those early weeks of the siege, many still held a shred of hope that the Russian forces would respect the rules of engagement and not go after vulnerable civilians. How naïve of us to believe in basic human decency.

There was also the option of running to the Cathedral of the Intercession of the Mother of God, located near Theater Square. The striking gold-domed structure took years to construct and was only recently finished. In childhood, I was very close to a Muslim girl who later moved to Kiev. When I showed her images of the finished cathedral before the war, she was taken by its beauty. "It's stunning, isn't it?" I asked her. "It's almost like your mosque, only with crosses on top."

The cathedral was positioned at one of the highest points in Mariupol, reaching a height of eighty-four meters—a sitting duck for the aerial bombing. I could only hope the breathtaking edifice would not be destroyed.

After a few days in the vestibule, our food supply ran out. Ukrainians shop differently than Americans. We don't stock up on food in preparation for the week ahead, nor do we buy in bulk; life did not stop at night. One could always find a round-the-clock pharmacy, restaurant, or supermarket. Most of the apartment buildings had supermarkets on the first floor or in neighboring apartment buildings. We would purchase enough groceries to take us through one or two days, at most. Now, all of the supermarkets were closed. Many had already been destroyed.

It was not easy to remain in close quarters with Luda and Ivan's dachshund either. Luda had found the dog on the street the year before. The old dachshund had congenital problems with her paws. The previous owner must have thrown her away like garbage. Sadly, Mariupol had many stray animals wandering about, which I considered unacceptable.

Life on the streets gave that dachshund a terrible temper. She was always barking. If you did not pay attention to her, she made a sound like a drill. Luda and Ivan regretted the day they picked up the dog and took her home. They went on vacation last summer and I offered to care for the old girl.

I took her on walks with Yola and paid a lot of attention to her. She behaved perfectly without Luda and Ivan around. They returned from vacation, amazed at the transformation. Within minutes, the dog returned to incessantly barking and sounding like a drill.

And so, we sheltered in that vestibule, with Yola silently cowering beneath my legs during the shelling, and Luda and Ivan's dog barking her brains out 24/7.

Neighbors told us there was a large shelter located beneath a Zhiguli auto parts store located on the first floor of Luda's apartment building. At least two hundred people were already hiding in the basement. We were in no hurry to go down to the shelter, however, as the neighbors had informed us it was damp, dirty, and without light. There was no heat either—an important necessity in the wintry month of February, when temperatures are usually below freezing.

My mind changed dramatically on March 4. It marked the day when the Russian offensive stepped up its game and mercilessly pummeled our section of the city. It was also Luda's birthday. We were tired of being stuck in the vestibule. The streets were relatively calm, so we decided to take a chance and return to Luda's apartment to drink coffee and eat the little bit of chocolate that remained in her pantry. It was hardly a celebration; it was more of a reprieve.

I sat in an armchair in their apartment with my back to the window. A shell suddenly hit the floor above us. All of the windows, including the one inches away from my back, blew out of their frames and smashed to pieces on the floor. The door from the balcony flew across the room with such force that it easily could have killed us if we stood in its path.

I fell to the floor and turned to see Yola running from room to room in fright. I lifted her eighteen-kilogram body and headed back to the vestibule between the apartments. Luda followed after us. Ivan was pulling his old dachshund out from under the sofa when the second explosion occurred.

Luda hysterically called out from the vestibule, "Ivan! Quickly, here!"

Ivan ran into the vestibule carrying the dog. His sweater was streaked with blood.

Luda rushed to him. "Are you all right?"

"I'm fine, I'm fine," he reassured her. A few small fragments of glass and metal had hit him but created surface-only abrasions.

We huddled together in the vestibule. The entire building shook from the explosion, its once sturdy walls like fragile matchsticks on the verge of collapse. The deafening roar of shelling surrounded us, and when I say deafening, I mean it was the loudest sound I have ever heard. I thought my eardrums would explode. I fell to my knees and covered Yola with my entire body. She was trembling all over and pressed into me with all of her weight. The poor animal. She did not understand what was happening.

"We need to run to the underground shelter," I told Luda.

"Wait until everything calms down," she said.

Ivan agreed. "Luda's right. Going to the shelter is suicide."

Ignoring them, I hastily leashed Yola and went to the door—but Yola refused to leave. She resisted moving, her body like a limp rag doll. Undeterred, I dragged her down the stairway by her leash. In the lobby, she instantly jumped into motion, ran across the carpet of broken glass, and fled into the street.

Chapter Five

The neighbors' bleak descriptions of the shelter were spot on. The massive basement was pitch black and damp. The concrete walls were crusted with mold. Puddles of filthy water covered the floor. It was unbearably cold. Close to two hundred people huddled in the darkened corners. In those early days, there was a buzz of conversations—people talking and even laughing, while others loudly wept and cursed, "Why would they do this to us? We pose no threat!"

It only took seconds for Luda and Ivan to realize that remaining in the vestibule was suicide and that fleeing to the underground shelter was a necessary course of action. They followed me, and together, we located an empty room in the shelter.

The winter season lasts for four months, from mid-November to mid-March. The coldest month is January, with an average low of negative 6°C and an average high of 0.5°C. I had fled my apartment wearing sweatpants, a sweater, a winter coat, and boots that provided a thin layer of insulation. The dank basement was an icebox. I constantly trembled with cold and embraced Yola for warmth.

I poured the contents of my backpack onto my lap and took an inventory of my food and supplies. I had brought a 2.5-kilogram bag of dog food from my apartment. Yola had already eaten one-third of it.

"How will I feed Yola when this kibble is gone?" I fretted to Luda. "All of the stores have been stripped bare by looters."

"There's a pet store at the corner of this building," Luda said. "Go see if there is any dog food left."

It was the middle of the afternoon. The fighting above us had briefly abated. I climbed the wooden stairway and ran with Yola to the pet store. The door was wide open. People were taking all they could carry from the shelves. I grabbed the last remaining bag of dog food. Although it weighed ten kilograms, the bag seemed light in my arms as I rushed out of the store and headed back to the shelter, a powerful rush of adrenaline shooting through my body. I had never run so fast in my life.

Early on, Yola whimpered to go outside and do her business. I didn't want her to urinate in the shelter, so I took her outside to go on the lawn. Suddenly, low-flying planes flew past, dropping bombs and destroying everything in their path. Panicked, I headed back to the shelter, but Yola got herself tangled around a bush. I desperately unraveled her leash from the twigs and pushed her through the doorway. We were lucky to have survived.

After that, we never left the shelter.

For my first three nights underground, I slept sitting up on my backpack rather than lying down in the puddles of stagnant water. Some men in the shelter risked their lives to retrieve rubber car mats, car batteries, and fire extinguishers from the shop upstairs. They returned with their bounty and laid the rubber mats over the wet concrete. From the car batteries and LEDs, the men created weak streams of light that allowed us to see one another's ghostly silhouettes.

I slept on the rubber mats, thankful to the men for their bravery. Those same men would go on to carry out many more sacrificial acts in which they put the needs of the shelter's inhabitants before their own. They generously shared their food with others when they first arrived, broke up quarrels, and intervened when people stole from one another. They also wrote the large inscription "PEOPLE 215 PEOPLE" on the street outside the shelter using spray paint to notify Russians that civilians were inside the basement. They were natural-born leaders intent on keeping order and lifting morale. Without them, our time in the shelter would have been even more difficult.

My phone had started to lose its connection when I hid inside the vestibule. I turned it off when I entered the basement because I wanted to save the remaining charge. It was a good decision; everyone's phones completely ran out by the second day, fueling our sense of helplessness and isolation. Some crafty people were able to charge their phones using two wires attached to the car batteries. However, others resented them for doing this, swearing at them for using up the energy in the batteries that provided us with light.

I stroked Yola's soft fur to quell the panic inside me. Few people went out into the street because of the nonstop shelling from Russian aircraft and equipment. Those who did leave did not fully realize the seriousness of the situation. Men would go outside for a smoke break; others fearlessly left to rob neighboring shops or return home to fetch their belongings. They assumed luck was on their side and they would not get hit by rapid aerial shelling. Sadly, many of them never returned. They were shot or hit by shelling in the streets and crawled to nearby buildings to die.

Our heads all ached from the loud booming. From the shelter's doorway, I would sneak peeks at the chaos outside. The building across from us was still standing. In the daytime, the windows reflected the sky and sun.

A rancid stench permeated the dank air since over two hundred people and their pets relieved themselves in specified corners. We had no buckets. Who thought about grabbing a bucket before leaving their homes during heavy bomb fire? Most of us had only the clothing on our backs.

We were forced to urinate and defecate on the floor. We were also running out of toilet paper. Mothers made do with torn pieces of comforters and blankets to diaper their babies. The unsanitary conditions contributed to all of us getting sick from the dampness and cold.

The population in the shelter mirrored that of the city as a whole. I conversed with people of all ages and from all walks of life: children, adults, and the elderly. Everyone reacted differently to what was happening. Some looted liquor stores and drank all of the time. Others were silent—almost meditative. Some very nervous people were prone to wringing their trembling hands, hyperventilating, whimpering, weeping, and whining. Children who were too young to understand what was happening ran about playing hide-and-seek. They would ask for my cell phone to play games. I told them my phone was shut off because I was saving the remaining charge in case of an emergency—an emergency, that is, in which someone on the other end of the line could do something to assist.

We talked about everything: who would win the war, how we would escape and where we would go, whether anyone would come to save us, what our lives were like before the war. Engaging in conversation allowed us to momentarily forget we were trapped inside that dreadful basement, but then a strong explosion would sound from above and everyone fell silent—even those who constantly whined.

Our leaders were optimistic and practical. They would laugh and tell jokes to boost our spirits. They would run into the street to retrieve items we needed when they felt it was relatively safe to leave. They reminded us to stay quiet, to only use a back section of the shelter to relieve ourselves, and to smoke in locations that were not beside the places where we slept.

The food ran out. For days, we starved. The fighting and shelling were constant. It was too dangerous to leave the shelter and retrieve food. We experienced nausea, stomach pains, and diarrhea. There were no doctors or essential medicines. Everyone was coughing and had sore throats; many had fevers.

I suspect COVID was spreading through the basement. The positivity rate was at its highest two weeks before the invasion began, with less than forty percent of the Ukrainian population vaccinated against the highly transmissible virus. Disrupted access to healthcare facilities, testing, and treatment meant conditions were ripe for the spread of the deadly virus in bomb shelters, trains, buses, and at border crossings where crowds of people huddled together.[6] As for the inhabitants of our dank shelter, no one wore face masks. We didn't have hot water or soap, and we were quickly running out of the drinking water that our leaders had drained from the apartment boilers.

Those who suffered the most were the elderly and small children whose immunity was low. A heavyset woman in the shelter was slowly dying before us. She had been without her insulin and other essential medicines for weeks. She vomited frequently. Her face was flushed, and her breathing was deep and fast. She complained of severe muscle stiffness and aches. There was an unnaturally fruity smell to her breath. We watched her suffer and felt utterly powerless to assist. Would I have survived such conditions if I was not healthy and young? I don't know.

Without any windows from which sunlight could flow, we lost all sense of time. We continued to pray for peace, hoping against hope that negotiations would succeed. A few people continued to risk leaving the shelter and ran back to their apartments to retrieve blankets, water, and food.

---

6. "5 health crises that endanger Ukrainian lives as the war continues." *International Rescue Committee.* 7 April 2022. https://www. rescue.org/article/5-health-crises-endanger-ukrainian-lives-war-continues#:~:text=More%20than%2090%20attacks%20on,Syria%2C%20 Yemen%20and%20other%20conflicts.

Those provisions rapidly diminished. Our empty stomachs groaned with hunger.

One afternoon, Russian soldiers entered our shelter. They arrogantly marched through the corridors carrying assault rifles at their sides. "If any of you are soldiers," one soldier shouted, "we will shoot everyone in this shelter!"

Give me a break, I thought angrily. *We are sick and starving and freezing. Most of us are women or children. Do we look like soldiers? Put down your guns and give us some food!*

Ear-splitting shelling occurred around the clock. It would usually die down around midday, from 11 a.m. to 4 p.m., although it was still unsafe to leave during that period. Shells sometimes dropped and the street fighting was constant. The shelling would increase aggressively as night approached. Just when you thought calmness would prevail, another shell would fly at the building or other tall buildings nearby, causing the walls above to sway and shake as the ground moved beneath our feet.

We could hear a full-scale battle in the streets above— the booming of heavy artillery, buildings collapsing, and gunfire crackling. Always, there was the sound of crying and groaning from the people underground—children, women, and even men.

One night, I heard Russian soldiers shouting at Ukrainian soldiers in the street above, "Surrender! Surrender!"

To which the Ukrainian soldiers replied, "Fuck off!" The Ukrainian soldiers were not afraid of death; they were not afraid of anything. My heart swelled with love and gratitude. Those brave warriors exemplified true courage.

A few of the leaders left the shelter and ran to a nearby warehouse in search of food. They returned with boxes of waffles and chocolate. For weeks, we survived on only waffles and chocolate, and we grew even sicker from malnourishment.

I lost a significant amount of weight on that diet. I don't care if I never eat another waffle again.

Chapter Six

One night, I awoke to a chorus of agonized screams sounding from the street above. A neighboring building had taken a direct hit. Bloodied people stormed into our basement shelter, their faces covered in dirt and shards of glass. They collapsed on their hands, yelling that the building they were hiding under was smashed by bombs dropped from Russian airplanes. They said that the entrance and walls of their shelter had collapsed on their heads. Dozens of people remained beneath the blockages.

A middle-aged man without a single scratch appeared in the doorway, his heart breaking from the stress. He clutched his chest, fell down the stairway, and instantly perished from a massive heart attack.

The condition of the survivors of that bombardment was critical. They begged us to save their family members trapped beneath the rubble, but not even our brave leaders were willing to go outside and rescue them. It was too dangerous. Fierce fighting was taking place in the street while bombs fell from above. Moreover, most of the bodies could not have been pulled out of the rubble without special equipment.

A few months before the invasion, a friend invited me to attend a week-long first-aid course given by the Malta Cross Foundation. It happened quite by accident. I was extremely interested in treating people in critical medical situations, and this opportunity serendipitously fell into my lap. Students were assigned mannequins with hypothetical injuries and were taught how to respond to a crisis quickly and calmly. At the time, I had no idea I would soon be utilizing the instruction in a war that would mirror Russia's ruthless attacks on Chechnya and Syria whereby indiscriminate bombing of residential roads and neighborhoods would result in massive civilian casualties.

A man had fled the carnage on a broken foot. The bones were protruding from his flesh. His leg shook uncontrollably as he slipped in and out of consciousness. I was one who kept others from bleeding to death from their wounds. I held my breath and forced myself to pull the blood clots from the man's wounded leg. The rancid odor of those clots disgusted me to the point of nausea. I had never witnessed so much blood.

A surge of adrenaline sharpened my mind and gave strength to my hands. I kept saying to myself, *Just think that this is meat on the counter, Adoriana. It's just meat, just blood, just bones. No, it is not a human being, and it does not hurt.* In this manner, I was able to use my bootlaces as a tourniquet and then bandage up the man's foot and leg. I believe I was meant to take that paramedic course in the autumn of 2021. The experience was not a coincidence. It carried a mystical purpose. I was destined to treat this man.

That poor soul was not the only person I treated. I pulled out shards of glass lodged beneath the skin of children and adults. I saw holes in skulls and protruding bones the color of dull ivory. I tried to stop the bleeding by plugging up wounds with any absorbent material I could find. I dressed lesions using improvised means—shirt sleeves, blankets, anything that was available. I also roused people who were losing consciousness. Some of the survivors of that blast had their fingers and limbs blown off.

It was a terrible night, a night when those of us who were still alive lost all hope that we would survive future attacks.

In the street above, the screams of those trapped inside the bombed-out shelter reverberated for hours. At some point, what remained of the building caught fire. All of the people pinned down by the mountain of debris perished in terrible agony. By morning, the screams had gone silent.

Some of the injured who fled the bombed-out shelter went on to die slow, agonizing deaths. We could not take their corpses out into the street. We slept next to them. As days passed, the corpses began to rot, emitting a putrid odor, smelling like fruity feces and spoiled meat. The unholy scents made us gag. All hope was lost. Would we be among the dead in the days to come?

Though I was completely exhausted, I rarely slept due to the ceaseless bombing. Imagine what it would sound like if a fast-moving train crashed into your house, followed by another train crashing into your neighbor's house, and you will understand how powerful the booming was—day after day, night after night.

I hugged Yola for warmth and comfort. I cupped her handsome face in my open palms, finding solace in her ice-blue eyes. I have always been fond of the husky breed. Two years before, I returned home to discover a furry little miracle waiting for me in a box in my living room. Vanko had purchased the puppy and wanted to surprise me. The happiness I felt when I first laid eyes on Yola was indescribable. It was completely without reason, similar to the overwhelming euphoria of romantically falling in love. God, it was wonderful.

Those familiar with the breed would tell me, "Huskies are not toys. You need to devote a lot of time to a husky. She will gnaw at everything in your apartment. No, the husky is not a breed for the home…."

Yola proved them wrong. I did not have any difficulties with her. She is an amazing, obedient, and devoted animal. The key is to treat a dog as you would want to be treated. If I needed to go somewhere, I would take Yola with me. I understood her need to communicate with humans and other dogs. Our love was reciprocal from day one.

There were people who did not take their pets with them when they evacuated at the start of the invasion. Dogs and cats were left without any chance of survival in empty apartments. Some dogs were left outside on chains. My heart grieves for them. I cannot wrap my brain around such cruelty. Since the start of the invasion, many strangers would ask me, "Why are you dragging your dog inside with us? Now people cannot get in."

Yola did not cause any problems, even during the heaviest and loudest shelling. She would stand silently beside me, completely terrified. Later, when we entered buses, she would hide under seats so as not to stick out. That dreadful time we shared in the shelter served to strengthen our bond. In the book, *Man's Search for Meaning*, Holocaust survivor Viktor Frankl writes about how men and women found the will to survive the daily horrors of Hitler's concentration camps. "Those who have a 'why' to live," according to Frankl, "can bear with almost any 'how.'"

In my case, Yola was my "why" to live in those desperate weeks buried beneath the auto shop. While part of me no longer cared if I lived or died, the part of me that loved Yola knew I had to maintain my strength and sanity to protect her. If anything happened to me, what would come of Yola? She would be helpless without me. In turn, Yola remained absolutely obedient in the face of great turmoil to protect me.

***

While some of the men in our shelter were heroes, others were villains.

I don't understand why good people die and some bastards live. A freak of a man, about fifty-five years old, had stolen alcohol from various shops and was constantly drunk. I was in a small room within the shelter where three of us—Luda, her husband Ivan, and me—hid with our dogs. The older man would always come to us, drunk, and ask, "Guys, can I sit with you?"

I instinctively disliked him. I did my best to ignore him, sometimes saying things to drive him away. Ivan chastised me, "Adoriana, he drinks. It doesn't mean he is a bad person. Let him sit. This is not your apartment. We are now in a public place. Let him drink. What do you care about him? He doesn't touch you."

Luda and Ivan smoke cigarettes. I don't smoke. One day, they went to another section of the shelter to smoke with others while I was alone in the room with Yola. The drunk man walked over and sat about a meter away from me.

He leered at me with lecherous eyes and began to ramble incoherently, "Why are you alone? Where is your man? Well, you want a man? You want me to fuck you?"

I told him to shut up and leave.

"Why are you talking to me like this?" he slurred. "I want you now. Let me just hug you...." He climbed on top of me, breathing his foul halitosis all over my face.

Luda's father made knives and leather goods. He was in the shelter with us, and he had given her one of his sharpest knives. Squirming beneath the drunk man, I managed to grab that knife from the floor.

"If you get close to me by even a millimeter," I screamed, "I will slice your neck! I will cut you to pieces and throw you into the street and nothing will happen to me for this!"

Yola barked furiously. Some of the leaders rushed over and took the drunkard away. When Luda and Ivan returned, they treated the matter like it was some kind of a joke. They laughed.

"Yes, he is completely drunk," Ivan said. "He wouldn't do anything to you."

Luda agreed. "He's just talking nonsense, Adoriana. "Don't be afraid of him."

Their callous responses made my blood boil. That drunk man surely would have raped me had I not threatened him with the knife and screamed loud enough for others to hear.

On another occasion, a fire broke out in the shelter. Those same good men who protected me from the drunk man broke through a door to another room and put out the fire. They were angels, not people. With exactly two hundred and seventeen people now stowed away in the shelter, we needed them more than ever...

Chapter Seven

I had been holed up underground for two weeks when the auto parts store above us took a direct hit from a projectile. The store caught fire. Smoke from burning paint, rubber tires, oil, and other noxious chemicals in the store poured into the shelter. I took one breath; the smoke instantly burnt my lungs. It felt like my eyeballs were pin cushions to hundreds of stabbing needles. Ahead, a panicked crowd of people ran to the exit, pushing for others to get out of the way.

I thought I would suffocate and die. I managed to push my way up the stairway and run into the street under heavy mortar shelling. It was 3 a.m. Outside, it was like Dante's Seventh Circle of Hell. A giant ring of tall buildings burned from top to bottom, their balconies thunderously crashing to the ground. Windows were flying out. I could hardly see through the thick reams of smoke. It was a shadowland of chaos. Everyone was screaming.

"Stop, don't go there!"

"The buildings are all on fire!"

"Let's find another entrance!"

"Where did you go? I see nothing in the smoke!"

"We need to run to the hospital and go under it!"

"No, not the hospital. We need to go under that building over there!"

I joined in the cacophony. "Luda, where are you?" I shouted. I located Luda through the dense plumes of smoke. She was headed in the direction of my apartment building. "Stop, Luda!" I shouted. "It's not safe over there!"

Russian soldiers either mistook us for saboteurs or did not care if they shot at civilians. After all, they had full knowledge of the presence of over two hundred civilians hiding in our underground shelter. They opened fire on our group. I saw a bright flash, followed by a loud explosion. I immediately fell to the ground and lay my face against the melting snow and broken glass. Shell fragments plastered my skin, and my ears were deafened instantly by a strong ringing in my head.

Time stopped in a strangely surreal way.

More high-pitched ringing.

More bright flashes from falling shells.

I heard Ivan shout so loudly that his voice broke in half: "Lie down, people!"

Of course, I was already lying down. Oddly, I felt no fear. Though I was surrounded by shelling and gunfire and shrieks of terror, only silence filled my ears. In a stupor, I squinted through the fog of smoke, unable to see the building under which I had hidden for the last two weeks. In that moment, I said goodbye to life.

But Yola had other plans. She was hooked to a leash that wrapped around my waist. As I lay on the ground prepared to die, Yola pulled with all of her strength and dragged me to the side of the road. I don't know what supernatural forces propelled me to then jump up and run—it was not my doing. I followed after Yola, unable to see where we were going. Yola located the blown-out auto parts shelter, entered through the door, and ran full speed down the stairway. I flew head over heels down the steps. Thankfully, I did not break any bones.

There were two doors at the foot of the stairway. One door opened into the shelter, from which thick, poisonous smoke still poured. The other door was locked. I hid in a corner as the noxious smoke rose above my head. I heard steps coming down the stairway, along with men's emphatic voices, followed by a loud crash. Our leaders had kicked down the locked door: it opened into a large closet with an electrical panel.

I was the first to rush into the closet. I heard the men run back to the street, shouting, "People, over here! Come down here!"

I was still in a stupor but quickly stirred as people flooded into the small room and squeezed in beside me. I don't know what was more terrible—the deafening explosions and the pervasive fear of death, or those heartrending cries of people dying in the street above. Probably the latter.

Not everyone in the street heard the men calling to them, "People, over here!"

More shells flew at the building and slammed the street-level entrance of the shelter. The men joined us in the small room. Had they not broken down the door, I would probably have perished at the foot of the stairway, as the canopy above the steps was a flimsy iron screen—a thin blanket of protection from enemy fire.

A woman ran down the stairway and called out for her child. She had lost him on the street. She stormed into the small room, screaming for her little boy. When she saw he was not there, she turned to leave.

One man grabbed her arm. "No," he said. "It's not safe up there."

The woman became hysterical. She pounded at the walls. She shrieked and sobbed, making no sense of her words. That little room became a miniature madhouse. I did not have enough air to breathe as more people entered and crushed me with their bodies. With my height of 160 centimeters (5'3"), they flattened me. I raised my head to try to catch a breath. Yola crouched at my feet, shaking all over.

It was impossible to hear individual shots firing in the street above. Rather, it sounded like a constant roaring rumble—the sound of thousands of bullets and shells being fired. The noise went on for the rest of the night. Despite the great number of people crammed together in that small space, I couldn't feel my legs and arms because of the extreme cold blowing in from the street.

At dawn, a man left the room and entered the main shelter to look for someone. He could not find the lost person. He returned to the closet and informed us that the store had completely burnt out from above and it was safe to return to the shelter next door. *Thank God*, I thought, *I can't bear to stand up for one more minute.*

The chemical smoke inside of the shelter gradually diminished, but the strong stench remained. I returned to the room where we had spent the last few weeks and took an inventory of my injuries. I had scratched my hands on broken glass; I had some bruises and abrasions. Otherwise, I was unharmed.

Chapter Eight

We were running out of water. In addition to draining water from the boilers, people were collecting droplets from the moldy pipes; others gathered dirty snow from the street during brief windows of time in which the fighting died down.

I was so thirsty that I could have chugged down a glass of vinegar if it was handed to me. The extremity of my thirst was indescribable—to wash down the snot, dust, and stink from my arid throat with a tall glass of water would have been heavenly. I closed my eyes and envisioned myself plunging into a pool of water and lapping it up like a dog or laying in a warm bathtub for an entire week and drinking gallons of ice-cold water from buckets. One afternoon, I plucked up the courage to leave the shelter and fetch five liters of water that remained in my apartment.

I headed in the direction of my building. Shelling and gunfire rumbled in the near distance. I dashed from building to building, stopping to hide in alleyways whenever explosions sounded. I peered around the corner like a mouse hiding from a cat, estimating with my ears where the shelling was coming from before I resumed running. My heart pounded wildly as I sprinted through lanes littered with scrap metal, dismembered human limbs in varying states of decomposition, and debris.

My phone dropped to the ground. As I turned around to retrieve it, a powerful explosion sounded nearby. *Do I need this phone or to hell with it?* I made a split-second decision to run back to the phone and pick it up. It was yet another choice that would one day save my life.

How to describe the ghastly hellscape? Burnt-out cars, some crushed by Russian tanks, some containing rotten corpses. Piles of shattered bricks and broken glass cluttered the ground. A billboard depicting bright yellow Ukrainian sunflowers framed by a cobalt blue sky was splattered with mud and blood. There was no time to take in the horror. I had to maintain focus and get to my apartment alive.

It felt like ages passed before I arrived at my final destination. I entered the building and vaulted the stairwell two steps at a time. I flew into the apartment. It was freezing inside. All of the windows had been blown out, even the interior glass doors that led to the balcony. My mother's hand-embroidered linen curtains flapped plaintively against icy gusts of wind blasting in from the Sea of Azov. Despite the architectural damage, I longed to remain in the apartment. I was terrified of getting killed on my trip back to the shelter and this, after all, was the only home I'd ever known.

Logic took over. I forced myself to leave the apartment, but not before grabbing a thick blanket, a heavier winter coat, and the precious five liters of water from the pantry. The tap water in Mariupol tasted awful. It was overchlorinated and tasted like pool water. Although it was said to correspond with safety standards, no one in their right mind drank it directly from the tap. Doing so made us sick to our stomachs. Instead, residents filtered or boiled tap water before drinking it. For this reason, there was a rocky coating on the bottom of our kettles and pots. I could not tolerate the taste of the water even after boiling it, so I used to purchase mineral water that originated from Morshyn or the Carpathians.

I did not realize just how hard Mariupol's water was until I visited the Carpathians, located in the southwestern corner of Ukraine, a few years ago. Out of habit, I poured a large handful of shampoo into my open palm when I showered. As I lathered the shampoo into my scalp, a helmet of foam instantly formed around my head. I could not believe the amount of suds the soft water created. Every time I rinsed it, more foam formed. After, it felt like my hair was cleaner and silkier than ever.

I clutched the plastic jug of mineral water to my chest as though it were the world's most expensive bottle of Dom Pérignon. I had been romancing that water in my mind for weeks. On the return trip, I ran past the Port City Mall. Once a pristine structure with a dazzling neon-blue façade, Port City was a place where residents could spend a leisurely afternoon browsing casual clothing shops like Tom Tailor and Levi's and celebrating purchases over a slice of New York Street Pizza in the food court. Now the mall was a high-value military target.

Emboldened by the success of my journey, I considered stepping into the vacant mall. *What if there is some food there? But how will I carry food in my arms with this blanket and jug of water?* Just then, a line of fast-flying bombs dropped onto a corner section of the mall. I froze in the middle of the parking lot, my eyes frantically searching for a bush or tree to hide behind. To say that it was an *epic situation* is no exaggeration.

I ran at what felt like the speed of light to the nearest building and crouched beneath the canopy. You can go online and see photos of the Port City Mall before the invasion and watch drone footage of what the relentless aerial shelling did to the mall. Such waste. The Russians are now occupiers of rubble—hideous, filthy rubble. *Russia has uglified my city*, I thought. Was *uglify* even a word? I looked it up on dictionary.com.

Uglify: to make or become ugly or more ugly.

Turns out, it was precisely the right word for what Russia did to Mariupol.

Months later, I would watch a video clip of Maria Pirogova, the deputy of the People's Council of the DPR, on the city website of Mariupol.[7] Paraphrasing, Pirogova said that Mariupol was defiled with beauty and parks, and now the city had been cleared of unnecessary tinsel. Imagine viewing parks and beautiful structures where people can congregate as objects of defilement—nothing more than cheap tinsel. I don't believe that an educated woman like Pirogova truly believed what she was saying—that Mariupol's once glorious landscape has been "restored" by Russia's uglification. Rather, she was willing to say anything to gain Putin's approval and climb the ranks of power.

I finally arrived at the shelter and nursed the water with Yola for several days. I took tiny sips from the plastic bottle and poured tablespoons into a dish for Yola.

Clean water—what bliss!

---

7. *The News of Mariupol.* https://www.0629.com.ua/news

Chapter Nine

I worried about the children in the shelter. Their faces were sallow, their eyes sunken and devoid of light. Their little bodies could not withstand the dramatic fluctuations in food and water intake. I was also concerned about the water we were drinking from the boilers and pipes. Contaminated water causes diarrhea, which escalates dehydration. Poor water quality can also cause outbreaks of communicable diseases. Mariupol suffered an outbreak of cholera in 2011, so the bacteria that causes cholera is still in the region.[8]

I am no expert on the issue, but based on what I read in news reports, I believe the outbreak was a result of factories that poured tons of dirty liquids and waste products into the sea. The fish died and harmful bacteria developed, including cholera. Our city was forever on the brink of ecological disaster because of the reckless habits of industrial enterprises. Rallies took place where hundreds of people carried posters that said WE HAVE NOTHING TO BREATHE. The protestors demanded the installation of cleaning filters, regulations on the manmade mountains of slag at industrial sites, and the overall production of waste.

At the time, I supported the protestors. We were all angry at Rinat Akhmetov, the richest man in Ukraine, who,

---

8. Intrefax-Ukraine. "Area in Ukraine Hit by Cholera Outbreak." *Kyiv Post.* 24 July 2011. https://www.kyivpost.com/article/content/ukraine-politics/area-in-ukraine-hit-by-cholera-outbreak-109266.html

as previously noted, owned the Astov Steel Plant. Akhmetov also owned many mining and metallurgical businesses in the region. Whenever he was slapped with environmental fines, he simply paid them off. With a net worth of almost six billion dollars, paying a hefty fine was the price of doing business—a minor nuisance, at best.

In my opinion, the Ukrainian oligarch did not care about the safety and welfare of the residents of Mariupol or the future of the planet. Akhmetov did not have to live in our polluted city. He was free to vacation at his $221-million villa in the French Riviera, travel to his $150-million apartment building in Hyde Park, London, or hop aboard his magnificent superyacht and sail the Sea of Azov.

In fairness, I should add that Akhmetov has emerged as a vigorous supporter of Ukraine in the war. He is presently deciding whether to sell Luminance, a 475-foot luxury vessel docked in a German shipyard, as a means of distancing himself from Russian oligarchs who also love their yachts.[9]

President Zelensky repeatedly visited Mariupol in the years leading up to the invasion. He wanted to transform Mariupol into a resort city. Under his sound authority, the local government began to question whether there were economic alternatives to having so many factories in the city. Corresponding plans were gradually implemented, with more environmentalists dropping into factories for surprise inspections.

Akhmetov was encouraged to move his enterprises outside of the city. Of course, such an endeavor was a utopian fantasy. Akhmetov's factories sprawled across miles of land. They did not exactly lend themselves to gentrification, and the cost of plowing them down and removing the debris was astronomical. Nevertheless, the younger residents were immensely thankful to Zelensky for his initiatives. Who

---

9. Forsythe, Michael. "Ukrainian Oligarch Seeks to Distance Himself From Russia by Selling of Superyacht." *New York Times.* 19 May 2022. https://www. nytimes.com/2022/05/19/world/europe/ukrainian-oligarch-superyacht.html

wouldn't want to popularize their city by opening new educational institutions and holding seasonal festivals? Who didn't enjoy breathing cleaner air?

Days passed. My five liters of mineral water ran dry. My clothes stuck to my body and stank of body odor and burnt plastic. I had a tickle in my chest all of the time and no amount of coughing would relieve it. The cold, the stink— it was horrible. Women inside the shelter complained that they could not stay there with their children. The chemicals would injure their young lungs. Some left and headed to the basement of a neighboring building. Battered and bruised, I chose to stay.

***

I endured many sleepless nights in the shelter wondering how a tragedy like this could befall a peaceful nation. From the start, Putin called the military operation a "liberation." What a joke. It was ruthless revenge on the unconquered. There was no preliminary evacuation of our citizens. Putin knew full well that reducing Mariupol to rubble would result in the deaths of thousands of innocent civilians. In short, he did not care.

There were even people in the city who supported Putin's invasion. Whether one supported the invasion or not, I don't think that any of us were prepared for the horrors that lay ahead. Months before the bombing, we were told on Ukrainian television that the city was completely prepared to protect civilians in the event of an attack. I recall seeing a video on the nightly news that showed a sparkling new "capital" shelter. It was clean and cozy inside, and the walls were decorated with Ukrainian ornaments. The only thing that was missing was a jacuzzi and a wet bar.

Most Russians did not seem to care about the impact an invasion would have on ordinary Ukrainian citizens. Their minds were saturated with propaganda aimed at insulting and dehumanizing all Ukrainians. Moreover, the crimes against humanity presently taking place in Ukraine are not reported to Russia's citizens. The Russian government goes to great lengths to hide the atrocities, withholding information about civilian deaths and military defeats while depicting their soldiers as heroes.

Without a doubt, Ukraine presently endures the toughest information war in history. Almost everything is falsified by Russian media—almost everything is refuted. I have not heard such nonsense from other sources, only from Russia. Russian journalists, if you want to call them journalists, say on television that the corpses in drone footage are actors faking death. The Russian state media contends the scenes showing dead civilians are a meticulously staged montage created to provoke Russia. At times, I want to scream, "How can you be so stupid? Why don't you have your own opinion? Open your eyes! Open your brains! For God's sake, throw away your TV!"

There is nothing new about Putin's methods of deception. History instructs that every genocide begins with a diabolically crafted propaganda campaign. In the early 1930s, Joseph Stalin's desire to replace Ukraine's farms with state-run collectives resulted in the *Holodomor*, a combination of the words meaning "starvation" and "to inflict death."[10] Close to four million Ukrainians died in the manmade famine. In an article titled "How Fake News Helped Hide Soviet Genocide in Ukraine," Gerogiy Kent writes:

> The deliberate starvation was only possible due to blanket
> Soviet censorship and the collaboration of a Western
> press corps in Moscow who enabled the crime to protect
> their own accretion and maintain access to the Soviet

---

10. Kent, Georgiy. "How Fake News Helped Hide Soviet Genocide." *Atlantic Council*. 29 June 2020. https://www.atlanticcouncil.org/blogs/ukrainealert/how-fake-news-helped-hide-soviet-genocide-in-ukraine/

elite. As the shadow of death spread across rural Ukraine, international correspondents in Moscow lined up to denounce isolated reports of famine as "fake news."[11]

Sadly, history now repeats itself. As I write this, I fear there will be a famine in Ukraine since the fields of grain are deliberately set on fire by Russian soldiers. The grain that was harvested has been removed, and the sale of vegetables and fruits to territories outside of those now occupied by Russia is forbidden. Russia boasts record harvests. They are based on looted Ukrainian grain.[12] I see news footage of Ukrainian farmers weeping as they cart their wheat in trucks and dump it into landfills. Again, such waste.

The *Holodomor* was Stalin's means of punishing independence-minded Ukrainians who posed a threat to his totalitarian authority. Soviet propaganda portrayed the victims as *kulaks*, wealthy and stubborn landowners who were standing in the way of Stalin achieving a proletariat utopia. The kulaks were repeatedly dehumanized, with Stalin stating they should be "crushed out like parasites or flies and their food given to those who deserved it."[13] To this day, the Russian government that replaced the Soviet Union has denied that the famine was a genocide, insisting it was related to natural causes.[14] Also to this day, Ukrainian parents instruct their children to leave no breadcrumbs on the table at the end of a meal, in memory of the famine.

11. Ibid.

12. Good, Keith. "Under Russian Fire, Ukraine Farmers Face Harvest Scramble." Illinois. *FP Farm Policy News*. 14 June 2022. https://farmpolicynews.illinois.edu/2022/06/under-russian-fire-ukraine-farmers-face-harvest-scramble/

13. Kiger, Patrick J., "How Joseph Stalin Starved Millions in the Ukrainian Famine" *History*. 16 April 2019. Ultimately, the great famine was self-defeating for its perpetrators. According to one historian, "It generated so much hatred and resentment that it solidified Ukrainian nationalism." https://www.history.com/news/ukrainian-famine-stalin

14. Ibid.

Taking a page from Stalin's playbook, Russia's modern-day, state-run media has contaminated the minds of the Russian masses, convincing ordinary citizens through lies and distortions that Ukrainians are brainwashed Nazis. Even our Jewish president is a Nazi, they absurdly assert. In late March 2022, Russia shelled the Drobytsky Yar Holocaust Memorial near the eastern Ukrainian city of Kharkiv. The memorial marked where an estimated fifteen thousand Jews were shot or pushed into mass graves by Nazi troops. Those who were still alive slowly died of exposure. The complex's most notable feature, a heavy black menorah, was destroyed by Russian bombs.[15]

If Putin holds great respect for the Jewish people, he has a peculiar way of showing it.

I understand that not all Russians support Putin and his regime. Many are afraid to dissent as it may lead to incarceration or death. I have a Russian friend who went to an organized rally against the war, and he was beaten by law enforcement. I saw a video on the internet of a little old Russian lady who had had an anti-war phrase written on her handbag and a blue-and-yellow ribbon tied around her head. She was accused of incitement, with law enforcement surrounding the harmless babushka and demanding to know why she wore ribbons with Ukrainian colors. It is all so pathetic.

There are also thousands of Russians serving prison time and suffering God knows what else for standing up to Putin

---

15. Zitser, Joshua. "Ukraine says 'Nazis have returned' as Russian shelling wrecks Drobytsky Yar- the 2nd Holocaust Memorial to be bombed during war." *Business Insider.* 26 March 2022. https://www.businessinsider.com/ukraine-russia-shells-drobitsky-yar-holocaust-memorial-kharkiv2022-3

See also: Boissonzault, Lorraine. "The World War II Massacres at Drobytsky Yar Were the Result of Years of Scapegoating Jews." *Smithsonian Magazine.* 15 December 2016. https://www.smithsonianmag.com/history/wwii-massacres-drobitsky-yar-were-result-years-scapegoating-jews-180961466/

by protesting his sadistic war.[16] To these brave Russian men and women, I say a heartfelt *blagodaryu vas*! Thank you!

16. Treisman, Rachel. "Russia arrests nearly 5,000 anti-war protesters over the weekend." *NPR.* 7 March 2022. https://www.npr.org/2022/03/07/1084967986/russia-arrests-more-protesters

Chapter Ten

One afternoon, a man arrived in a car battered from shelling to search for his wife and six-year-old daughter. He ran down to the shelter and located his family. The wife had lost all hope that anyone would come to rescue them, especially since she had no mobile connection. I envied her. *She is so lucky*, I thought. *It's a pity that no one will come for me.*

The mother and daughter were beautiful—their creamy skin smooth as porcelain, and cheeks still rosy with health. The little girl wore a bright pink winter coat. Her hair was pale yellow, the color of wheat. They all hugged and wept for a long time. They were so thankful to be together again. The father promised that he would save them. He told his wife they needed to leave the city right away.

They left the shelter and went out to the street. They all got into the battered car and drove a few meters ahead. The people down below heard a great explosion. The young family had driven over an anti-tank mine. We could see the carnage from the shelter's open door. The passengers were ripped to pieces.

I stared in horror at the dismembered body of that little girl, torn inside out, hanging from the car door. Her flaxen hair was sprayed with blood. Her bloodstained pink coat hung from the door frame. That grisly image is permanently stamped in my mind. Looking at that dead child, I felt helplessness, rage, and a blinding sense of injustice. I wanted to shout to the whole world, "God, what have we done to deserve this hell on Earth? Ordinary people who have never taken up arms, people who live in their native land!"

In the days that followed, I fell into a state of abject despair. Whenever I climbed a few steps to look out the door, I would see a great mound of scrap metal and glass beside the battered car containing the bloody limbs of that young family. The explosion was so strong that the windows from the building across the street had flown out. Now I would no longer be able to look at the sun and sky mirrored in the glass.

My world was growing darker by the day.

Chapter Eleven

"At grief so deep the tongue must wag in
vain; the language of our sense and memory
lacks the vocabulary of such pain."
—Dante Alighieri, *Inferno*

Five weeks into the invasion, the relentless explosions and gunfire diminished. Russian soldiers had captured our area and moved their offensive to the center of the city. Now that most of the soldiers and tanks had moved on, we had a better chance of escape. People in the shelter began to discuss how they would do it.

We were all caught between the proverbial rock and a hard place. On one hand, leaving the shelter posed many risks—it was extremely cold outside, snow was flying, everyone was weakened, landmines littered the streets, and intermittent shelling was still taking place. On the other hand, the building above us was completely burnt out and could collapse like a house of cards at any moment. Great slabs of steel and concrete would fall on our heads, and there would be no one to rescue us from beneath the ruins. Even if the building remained standing, we were all starving and sick.

One of the first people to risk escape was a young mother with a four-month-old daughter. The baby was burning up with a fever. She had been crying for days and nothing could calm her down. The mother scooped the wailing infant into her arms and told us that she planned to walk to a village outside of the city. Under ordinary conditions, the village was a one-hour drive away. She left, taking the few glass jars of baby formula remaining. With the frigid temperatures and landmines everywhere, I have no way of knowing if she made it to that village.

A man from a neighboring shelter ran to us and said that a car transporting water had arrived across the street. People grabbed hold of empty bottles and left to fetch the water. They returned empty-handed. "We need buckets," they said. "The water is frozen."

"We have no buckets," one leader replied. "Everyone, find some big bags!"

People scurried around in search of bags. They handed them over and a few people went out to the car and returned with slabs of ice in the bags. More people left the shelter, bags in hand, but the shelling resumed. They were forced back to the shelter before retrieving any ice.

Other groups formed and fled. I too began to contemplate leaving the shelter for good, but I was so sick and weak with hunger. Just as I will never forget the ghastly site of that poor little girl hanging from the car door, I will also not forget the kindness of one woman at the height of my sickness. I had a high fever and was slipping into delirium. This kind woman gave me the last pills she had to treat my fever. It was a very emotional moment for me. She was also sick, but she placed my needs before her own.

The medicine brought my temperature down for only one day. By morning, the burning heat returned to my reddened cheeks, and I shivered uncontrollably. I clutched Yola for warmth, shut my eyes, and slipped into a hallucinatory reverie. In this state, I saw myself running with Yola along a verdant forest path. Everything was fine. The air was clean. There was no shelling, no gunfire—only peace. I felt so alive.

When I opened my eyes, I looked around and saw only death. The man with the broken leg that I had wrapped weeks before groaned loudly inside a room where the drunk pervert also stayed. The corpse of the man who had perished from a heart attack four weeks ago still lay in the corner. Through the open doorway, the little girl's bloodstained pink coat fluttered pitifully in the wind.

I turned to Luda and Ivan. "We will all die here. No one will save us. We must run away. If there is a chance to escape, then we must take that chance."

Luda answered, "Adoriana, my husband's father does not want to leave. We won't go without him!"

I glanced at the overweight woman who suffered greatly without her essential medicines. She huddled in the corner, half-conscious and shaking from the cold, moaning in pain. Her face and eyeballs had turned a pasty shade of yellow. It was clear to me that she would not survive much longer. Her plight strengthened my resolve.

I turned to Ivan. "There is a hospital nearby," I said. "We can steal a wheelchair and return it to Luda's parents. What difference does it make if we stay or go? Either way, we risk death."

"Even if we find a wheelchair for my father," Ivan argued, "we still have no place to go."

"I heard people talking about a refugee camp outside of the city," I replied. I knew my ideas sounded crazy to them. They sounded crazy to me too. I told them I was also afraid of running from the shelter, but we had no other choice.

Luda and Ivan finally gave in and agreed to run with me to the hospital. We had been hiding beneath the auto parts store for one month and two days. On March 27, 2022, we stepped outside of the shelter for the last time. I stood in shock, surveying my surroundings beneath the merciless glare of a cold winter sun.

The devastation was so much worse than it had been when I left the shelter to retrieve water from my apartment weeks before. How to describe what I felt? I have always loved springtime in Mariupol—the emergence of birds and flora, street festivals, music. Now, I saw my beautiful city razed to rubble. I had no emotions at that moment—not fear, not hatred, not sadness. I felt nothing. I was a complete vacuum.

Only one building remained standing in a neighborhood where nine- and fourteen-storied buildings once lined the streets. I couldn't see the street beneath my feet. It was carpeted with layers of scrap metal, shells, cartridges, fallen trees, and pools of blood. The landscape was also a meat grinder, with pieces of human bodies strewn over rubble every five meters.

Russia now occupied about ninety-five percent of the city. Russian soldiers were intent on sweeping away all traces of civilian deaths; I later heard that they were forcing residents to bury the corpses and dismembered bodies in exchange for a small piece of bread and a cup of water. I did not witness that, although I saw many yards where residents had dug holes with shovels and buried their loved ones, marking the graves with crudely constructed crosses made from tree branches. Russian soldiers were known to pull crosses from the mounds of dirt to erase their crimes.

After satellite photos revealed mass graves in Bucha, thereby exposing Russia's slaughter of civilians to the world, Russian soldiers began to dump corpses beneath a highway overpass in Mariupol and burn them in crematoria. Russian forces also took many bodies to a large shopping center, where there were storage facilities and refrigerators.[17]

To this day, outsiders remain desperate to find out if their loved ones trapped in Mariupol are alive and well. The silence of the missing is profound. Today, there is a Facebook page, "Missing Mariupol Residents," with more

---

17. Associated Press. "Mariupol Mayor Says Siege Has Killed More Than 10k Civilians." *US News.* 11 April 2022. https://www.usnewscom/news/world/articles/2022-04-11/ukrainian-defenders-dig-in-as-russia-boosts-firepower

than nine thousand members—all posting photos of missing family members and friends.

I moved past the battered car containing the corpses of the young family. Their limbs were bloated in an early stage of decay. Blood-smeared foam leaked from the child's mouth and nostrils. *Turn your eyes away. Staring won't help.*

As we headed in the direction of the hospital, I saw mountains of dead Russian soldiers and destroyed tanks and equipment marked with the letter *Z* cluttering the streets. Ironically, the white *Z*s, stylized with a thick brush stroke on Russian helmets and tanks, invoked Hitler's swastika in my mind— a pointless symbol for a pointless war.

The army of Putin and Kadyrov is not so invincible, I thought. *They are show-offs who bit off more than they could chew. Did they think we would welcome them with flowers and parades? Ukrainians are strong and proud people. Most would prefer death over submission to a totalitarian regime.*

The DPR had changed most of the road signs from Ukrainian to Russian. I later learned that a statue had been placed in Mariupol depicting an elderly woman grasping the Soviet flag. When asked about it, Petro Andrushchenko, an adviser to the elected mayor of Mariupol, bitterly stated that the Russians had "opened a monument made of shit and bricks to an old lady with a flag on Warriors Liberators Square, which they stubbornly call the Leninist Komsomol."[18]

I was stupefied by the complete decimation of the city's infrastructure. Before the invasion, Mariupol was an incredibly convenient city. I did not own a car, but that was never a concern. Everything was within a five-minute walk: hospitals, schools, supermarkets, which were open around the clock on weekdays, and outdoor farmers markets

---

18. Lister, Tim, Voitovych, Olga, and Presniakova, Julia. "From Medals to Road Signs, Russians try to put their stamp on Mariupol" *CNN*. 16 May 2022. https://www.cnn.com/europe/live-news/russia-ukraine-war-news-05-06-22/h_0 3a80de382043e695c834ced1760bfb0

in warmer weather. We had many convenient services that were not available to many Europeans. For example, Nova Poshta provided the fastest delivery of parcels in Ukraine—the equivalent of FedEx or UPS in America. A parcel from Kiev could be received in one day.

We could also easily purchase medicine at the pharmacy or order delivery, which would be received within a half hour. We did not have to wait for years to get an appointment with the doctor, and apps such as Diya stored all of our documents in digital form. Diya made it very easy to complete applications for government services and the like. Almost every shop closed or offered reduced hours on weekends. However, if you ran personal errands on weekdays, it was not a disruption.

I used to work out at the Terrasport gym. It was a great establishment with excellent trainers. The large building was used as a shelter at the start of the invasion. Now I saw it had been destroyed by bombs.

Tears stung my eyes. I looked at the wreckage of a sophisticated infrastructure that no longer existed. I wondered how residents who chose to stay would be affected in the years to come. Once home to about four hundred and thirty thousand residents, Ukrainian officials speculate that about one hundred thousand civilians now remain in the city. According to Mariupol's mayor, over twenty thousand Mariupol civilians have died in the siege, by May 2022.[19] How many more people would perish in the weeks and months ahead due to the loss of electricity, grocery stores, hospitals, and pharmacies? How many would grow sick in a filthy environment in which rotten corpses carpeted the streets?

---

19. Sullivan, Becky, Wamsley, Laurel. "Mariupol has fallen to Russia. Here's what that means for Ukraine" *NPR.* 19 May 2022. https://www.npr.org/2022/05/18/1099chapter885151/mariupol-falls-ukraine-russia-what-it-means

We plodded across the ruinous landscape and headed for the hospital. The city had an *end of the world* ambiance. People were burning damp tree limbs and cardboard boxes in smokey fire pits. Their faces were gaunt and covered in dirt, their hollowed-out eyes bereft of emotion. *They have no more tears left to cry,* I thought.

The stores had all been looted by Russian soldiers and Ukrainian civilians. Skinny stray dogs skittered about, sniffing at dismembered human limbs in search of food. In one parking lot, corpses of civilians were loaded into trucks. I sadly accepted the fact that Mariupol as I knew it would never exist again. According to the mayor, Vadym Boychenko, ninety percent of the infrastructure was destroyed by Russian forces, and at least forty percent of that was "no longer recoverable."[20]

We approached the hospital and suddenly froze in our tracks. Hundreds of people gathered in the block ahead. We were told this was the queue for evacuation. The large crowd was waiting for the buses. Since our phones had stopped working one month earlier, we had no idea evacuations were taking place.

Seeing that crowd and knowing we could finally leave took our breath away.

20. Chowdhury, Maureen, Hayes, Mike, Kurtz, Jason, et al. "Mariupol Mayor says 40% of city's destroyed infrastructure is no longer recoverable" *CNN*. 26 April 2022. https://edition.cnn.com/europe/live-news/ukraine-russia-putin-news-04-06-22/h_7c8bc8020669ba9eba20363afdbc5831

Chapter Twelve

We arrived at the hospital and signed up for queue 974. The Russian military occupied the entire building. A large Soviet flag stood outside the entryway. We located a rickety old wheelchair in the hallway and rolled it outside.

A Russian soldier stopped Ivan and grabbed the wheelchair. He gave us a long, hard stare. A contemptuous smirk tugged at his lips. "Where are you taking this?" he demanded.

Ivan and Luda explained the situation with Ivan's father. The soldier grudgingly allowed them to take the wheelchair and fetch Ivan's parents.

I stayed behind with our dogs and backpacks. I breathed a great sigh of relief when Luda and Ivan finally returned with Ivan's parents in tow. How they were able to roll that wheelchair carrying Ivan's father over all the ruins and debris remains a mystery.

Wounded Russian soldiers were staying in rooms situated in parts of the hospital that weren't burnt out by earlier shelling. We asked a group of soldiers if we could spend the night before evacuating the following day. They agreed we could stay on the eighth floor. You may think that this allowed us a small amount of respite, but the hospital was not much better than the shelter. We stayed in the wards where seriously ill COVID patients were treated before the war. The windows were all blown out. Shattered glass was everywhere. Folders containing patients' case histories were strewn across the floor, covered in the piss and shit of Russian soldiers.

You may also think that I was finally able to take a shower, but there had been no running water in Mariupol since the invasion began. I stank. Everyone stank. I had not brushed my teeth or hair for over a month. It was a bitingly cold night. The broken window frames rattled in the frigid wind. I found a lighter and made my way through the darkness to a closet in hopes of finding linens to keep us warm. There were only flasks and tubes.

I heard from others that a phone connection sometimes occurred near the tower of the Kyivstar mobile operator in the city center, so I finally turned on my phone. In the middle of the night, a text miraculously appeared from one of my friends who was fighting for Ukraine. He wrote:

GET OUT OF THE CITY TODAY OR TOMORROW. AFTER THAT, THE CITY WILL BE CLOSED AND THERE WILL BE NO WAY OUT. REMOVE EVERYTHING THAT IS ON YOUR PHONE, ESPECIALLY ANYTHING THAT HAS TO DO WITH MARIUPOL.

Wise words from a wise man. His advice gave me the determination to get out of the city straight away. On the morning of March 28, I waited with other evacuees in a long line that led to several dilapidated buses parked beside the hospital. I had expected to see the same buses that were recently purchased by our mayor, Vadym Boychenko, using money from the city budget. The sleek new vehicles were brought into the street when the war began for the purpose of evacuating civilians if the city was invaded. I learned those buses were quickly smashed to pieces by aerial shelling in the early days of the invasion.

My heart pounded wildly in my chest. Standing in that line and boarding a bus under Russian supervision frightened me more than the nonstop shelling when I was underground. I suppose it was the decisiveness of the moment that brought so much terror. The trip would take three days, and during that time, we would be under Russian command. Once I left Mariupol, there was no turning back.

Ivan and Luda weren't helping my stress levels. Ivan angrily cursed his parents for carrying a six-liter bottle of water. They in turn cursed Ivan and Luda for wanting to bring their old dachshund onto the bus. When the doors of the first bus opened, everyone began to aggressively push ahead and climb onto the bus despite the presence of a Russian soldier standing at the entrance with a machine gun. Enraged, the soldier lifted his gun and shouted, "Get back!"

No one appeared to hear him. We all had a singular and urgent goal—to step onto that bus and get the hell out of Mariupol. A fellow passenger later told me that the bus driver had said, "You don't need to come here with the dog," as I brushed past him. Fortunately, I did not hear him. That incident taught me an important lesson, however: feigning deafness or ignorance can be a resourceful strategy when faced with a threat.

The soldiers loaded Ivan's disabled father onto the bus with great difficulty. They could not figure out how to fold the wheelchair we'd stolen from the hospital. They swore and shouted at each other. There were very nervous men. Although I felt no pity, I could see the war was taking a toll on them.

We were cramped together as though sardines in a can. I dropped to the bench and struggled for breath. There were bags of personal belongings inside my jacket, and a large portion of Ivan and Luda's bags rested against my belly and lap. The doors closed shut and the engine revved. *It's happening,* I thought. *It's finally happening.*

But it was not happening. Not yet.

The soldier with the machine gun stood behind the bus and shouted to the driver, "The trunk won't close! It's too full of luggage and things!"

Equally frustrated, the driver shouted back, "Throw everything away! Otherwise, I won't go!"

The Russian soldier tossed plastic bags, carts, miscellaneous objects, and luggage from the trunk of the bus. Fortunately, my knapsack and a few other small bags were with me on the bus. I stared at the objects that had been dumped from the trunk onto the street. It occurred to me that it is heartless to criticize someone for wanting to hang onto a meaningful possession. What one individual sees as worthless or comical, another individual can deeply value. I saw in the underground shelter, and also on that bus, how grandmothers insisted on carrying along chipped porcelain dishes, teapots, and pillows. A mother yelled at her son for putting boxing gloves in his bag. One man's trash is another man's treasure.

As the bus slowly moved forward, I looked back at the long line of civilians who did not share my good fortune. They stared at the bus, emptiness and despair darkening their eyes. I felt guilty.

It took fifteen minutes for the bus to reach the highway exit leading out of Mariupol. That brief window of time offered a horrific excursion in which I saw the full extent of the burned and ruined buildings scattered throughout the city. To say Mariupol looked like hell on Earth is no exaggeration.

The bus headed in the direction of Nikolske, a town of about 2,800 people situated in the industrial sector of the Donbas. A sea of red Russian flags and paraphernalia ominously greeted us as we entered Nikolske. The flags hung from every single one of the trees that lined the streets and draped administration buildings and schools. Garish white Zs signifying WESTERN DISTRICT were painted on buses and cars. Russia certainly did not spare any money for its propaganda.

The Russian soldiers placed us in a school for two days. "If any of you are soldiers," they said, "we will shoot everyone in this room!"

We knew they meant it. There was a stark difference between the Russian soldiers in Mariupol and those we encountered in the Donbas. The ones who fought in Mariupol appeared to be relatively well-trained. Their ages ranged from eighteen to forty-five, with most of them in their late twenties, thirties, and forties.

The soldiers in DPR-held regions, like Nikolske, were the exact opposite. They behaved like the vicious boys who threw stones at Lassie. They were weak, young guys. Some of them looked like they were barely old enough to shave. They did not even have normal uniforms—some wore sneakers, others had shirts and pants that were a few sizes too big. They were a rabble of losers, mean-spirited and arrogant, treating all of this like some kind of game.

We were forced to undergo dehumanizing examinations at the checkpoints. The soldiers ordered the men to completely undress. They inspected every centimeter of their skin for tattoos indicating affiliation with the Ukrainian Army. Although I am a tattoo artist, I have no tattoos on my body, least of all any tattoos indicating military affiliation. My lifestyle before the invasion was notably apolitical. I never participated in rallies and parades.

In addition to inspecting our arms and legs for Nazi and pro-Ukrainian insignia, the soldiers took our fingerprints. They told us to turn over all of our data, including our phones. This process is different from the filtering that took place before Ukrainians were taken into Russia. In those situations, a facility like a police station or another government building was used to interrogate individuals more aggressively. For example, at filtration stations, husbands and wives were separated and asked the same questions. The Russian soldiers would then compare the answers for consistency. They asked questions like, "Where are the military facilities located in Ukraine? Why are you leaving Ukraine? How and why did the war start? Who caused it to happen?" According to people I knew who ended up in Russia, the ones interrogated had to toe the line and agree that the war was caused by Ukrainian Nazis.

For those of us who refused to go to Russia, passing the bodily inspection, and data and document approval allowed us to walk around the city. We were also promised safe passage to Rostov or Donetsk, both Russian territories within Ukraine.

My heart sank. There were no buses headed in the direction of western Ukraine. If I boarded a bus heading east, I would never be free again. Although I patiently endured the ridiculous procedures, the last thing I wanted was to live in a country stuck in the Stone Age—a country that sent her military to kill us.

Luda, Ivan, and his parents decided to board the bus headed east. I refused. They were incensed. Luda shouted, "Adoriana, it is because of people like you that the war continues!"

Ivan chimed in, "The Russians have made us a good offer. They promise benefits and food. They will resettle us."

I scoffed, "You must be joking! When you arrive, they will take away your passports and give you a piece of paper stating that you do not have the right to leave Russia. They will tout you as less than human. For the rest of your lives, you will be perceived as former Nazis that have been freed by Russia's bogus liberation. They will watch you like hawks. You will never be free again!"

"Shame on you, Adoriana!" Ivan shouted. "We must give these lands to the strongest and not get in the way of God!"

I stared at them in absolute shock. Were they willing to partake in Putin's Big Lie? What about all we had been through—the massacre we had witnessed with our own eyes? My mother and father still lived in Ukraine. By stepping on that bus, I would not only betray my country, I would betray my parents.

Luda and Ivan cursed at me, saying horrible, traitorous words. Tears flowed down my cheeks upon realizing these people whom I'd considered friends had joined the ranks of the enemy. I later heard reports about Russian filtration camps, where Ukrainian refugees and aid volunteers are subject to brutal interrogations involving shock treatment, beatings, and torture.[21]

As for Luda and Ivan, it's hard for me to care if they wound up at one of those camps. Although I share this story with you now, I have otherwise erased them from my mind.

21. Stanton, Andrew. "Russians Torturing Ukraine Aid Volunteers in 'Filtration Prison': Report." *Newsweek.* 17 May 2022. https://www.newsweek.com/russians-torture-ukraine-aid-volunteers-filtration-prison-1707354

Chapter Thirteen

The bus departed, leaving a trail of exhaust in its wake. I was left standing alone on the sidewalk with no place to go. I located a set of steps and collapsed in despair. An attractive middle-aged woman approached me. Her name was Natalia. She wore a modest grey dress that would have benefited from a colorful accessory, perhaps a floral print Slavic shawl or head scarf. However, in an occupied territory, a Slavic head scarf could get a woman killed.

What Natalia's wardrobe lacked in color, her face rectified. Her eyes sparkled like pools of water beneath a clear blue sky. Her plump lips were painted bright cherry red, and her smile was like the morning sun.

Natalia saw how I wept. "Why do you cry?" she asked. "What happened?"

I told her about my exchange with Luda and Ivan. Without hesitation, Natalia told me I could spend the night at her home and stay as long as I wanted until I decided what to do next. She was yet another angel I encountered during the war. She received me with all of the warmth and kindness that a good-natured person can give to another human being. She took me to her luxurious-yet-cozy house and accepted me as her own.

My gracious hostess was a widow with two children. Her adult son was married and lived in Georgia, and her younger daughter, Nina, lived at home. I'll never forget the look of worry that etched Nina's pretty face when I entered her home. She stood in the next room and peered at me anxiously through a crack in the doorway.

"Don't be afraid, Nina," Natalia told her. "Come meet our new guest."

Natalia gave me some of Nina's clothing and clean underwear. I cannot tell you how great it felt to remove my muddy sweatpants and sweater, my sullied undergarments and socks, and dress in lightly used hand-me-downs. Even after Natalia washed my old garments, they still stank of chemicals and gunpowder. Since she had no shoes to offer me, I was forced to wear my squalid boots. The leather and insoles had somehow absorbed the smell of the bloody hell pit beneath the auto shop. The laces were still streaked with blood from being wrapped around the leg of the wounded man as a makeshift tourniquet.

My parents raised me to understand the importance of hard work and self-sufficiency. It was therefore very difficult for me to enter Natalia's home with nothing to give her in return. I was extremely embarrassed by my circumstances.

I took my first shower since the invasion began. I spent three hours in that bathroom. I disrobed and stepped on the scale. I am 160 centimeters (5'3") in height. Before the invasion, I weighed 65 kilograms (143 pounds). Now, I weighed 56 kilograms (123 pounds). In the space of five weeks, I had lost twenty pounds through intermittent starvation, broken up only by chocolates and stale waffles. It is a weight-loss program I would never recommend.

Natalia had purchased a toothbrush for me. I scrubbed my teeth and flossed. My gums were red, sore, and very swollen. I spit mouthfuls of blood and plaque into the sink.

I stepped into the shower. The hot water had a way of opening up all of my wounds. I stood under the showerhead for at least ten minutes and bawled like a helpless child. I ran a soapy face cloth over my scratched and bruised limbs and vigorously scrubbed behind my ears and between my toes.

I could not believe this was happening to me. It seemed I had been thrust into a horror movie and I was now washing the nightmare away. I massaged shampoo into my scalp and watched as clumps of loose strands fell to the drain.

I stepped out of the shower and attempted to comb out the knots in my long blonde hair, but the strands were all tangled from weeks of not being maintained. I stared at the image of the haggard hippie with filthy dreadlocks reflected in the steam-covered mirror. I wondered how homeless people went without showering and clean clothing for months at a time. I looked like a train had run me over. I returned to the shower and washed my hair again, adding another layer of conditioner and lathering it through the knots.

As I stepped out of the shower a second time, Natalia knocked on the door. "Adoriana, are you all right?" she asked. "Will you have some soup?"

Her simple words—*will you have some soup*—brought tears to my eyes. Everything Natalia said broke my heart with such sorrow, such gratitude. Earlier, she had said, "Take hair balm to your tangles," and that sent me into a flurry of tears. I existed in parallel universes: one, in which great suffering and violence existed, and the other, a universe of compassion and infinite grace. I still had a high fever and nothing made sense.

"In a few minutes," I replied. I did not want to leave the bathroom. I was in a state of shock. Days before, I was trapped underground, having endured over a month of heavy warfare. Now, it was as if nothing had happened. How was it that I was suddenly safe? I was physically and emotionally fragile. At any moment, I would unexpectedly burst into tears. My brokenness frightened me. I did not want to burden Natalia with my pain.

I smothered my dry skin with body lotion and styled my hair. I emerged from that bathroom looking like my former self, albeit twenty pounds lighter. Nevertheless, no amount of grooming could restore my mind to the balance it possessed before the invasion. Memories of what I saw and experienced in Mariupol followed me like a dark cloud threatening turbulent storms.

I dressed in my new-to-me, lightly used set of clothes, and walked to the kitchen. Natalia stood before the stove, ladling homemade chicken soup into a bowl. She placed it on the table alongside a plate holding two thick slices of braided paska bread and a glass of cold milk. I dutifully took a seat at the table.

"How are you feeling?" Natalia asked.

I stared at her with red-rimmed eyes. My hand trembled as I dipped the spoon into the soup. I feared that the upset churning inside of me would explode at any second.

Seeing my distress, Natalia rose from her chair and gently laid her hand on my shoulder. "It's best for you to calm down and eat your soup in private," she said quietly.

A wave of relief swept over me. There was no way I could have swallowed the soup and bread in her presence. My throat was constricted, my stomach was in knots, and I was extremely self-conscious. As soon as Natalia left the room, I hoed into the flavorful soup containing chunks of white chicken, shredded cabbage, and thinly sliced garlic dill pickles. I could tell that Natalia had not scrimped on the ingredients. She used butter rather than lard, and sprigs of fresh parsley and thyme. I took a large bite of the Easter bread. It tasted citrusy, like the paska my mother used to make.

I mopped up the remaining broth with the last slice of bread and washed the meal down with milk. For the first time in five weeks, I felt satiated.

***

Nina was a talented violinist. The poignant music she performed for me on her Stradivarius violin helped to calm my agitated mind. I was also fascinated and impressed by the fact that such a fragile creature was at the top of her class in kickboxing.

Later in the afternoon, Natalia called Nina into the room and asked if she would go with me and Yola for a walk around the neighborhood; Nina agreed to join me and Yola. Within minutes, we were chatting like good friends. We returned and Natalia suggested that Nina take me to the store. She was quick to agree. How wonderful it was for Natalia to trust me with her daughter.

When we returned from our walk, Nina and I sat down at the long mahogany table in Natalia's dining room and Natalia served us a home-cooked meal. We ate dinner together every night during my stay in Nikolske, just like a close-knit family.

I wish I could say that I slept like a baby at Natalia's house, having endured so many sleepless nights. Though the bed was comfortable and the house was silent, I could not sleep because of a deep cough that sent me into a choking fit whenever I lay down.

On my first night in Nikolske, Nina appeared in the doorway. "It's late, Adoriana. Why don't you asleep?"

I told her about my chronic cough. What I did not say was the cough wasn't the only reason for my sleeplessness. I could not quiet my mind. To this day, I cannot stabilize my sleep. I wake up in the middle of the night and cannot fall back asleep. I have trouble falling asleep. I often have nightmares, most involving running from the shelter under heavy shelling and gunfire. During the day, I collapse with fatigue and nap, throwing my body into a vicious cycle of insomnia and fatigue.

On that evening, Nina gently took my hand and led me to the living room. "Let's work on some puzzles," she said softly. She prepared a cup of herbal tea for me and together, we worked on putting the pieces of the puzzle together. It was the perfect distraction.

If Natalia or her daughter were worried about catching my illness, they certainly did not show it. In the nights that followed, Natalia would awaken at all hours if she heard me coughing and gasping for breath. She wiped the perspiration from my brow with a wet cloth and gave me hot tea and medicine.

Sweet Natalia was a Ukrainian Florence Nightingale.

Chapter Fourteen

I learned from some people in Nikolske that there was a field outside of town with a tower allowing a mobile connection. I was finally able to phone my parents.

"Adoriana, how can we help?" my mother asked. "Come stay with us if you want. We are safe in our village. No one will touch us. There are no military facilities here."

I was shocked by her naïveté. "Don't you understand?" I asked in exasperation. "There are *no* safe places in Ukraine anymore. This is not a war on military facilities, Mom— *it's the destruction of everything alive! We all need to leave Ukraine.* Go anywhere, Mom—just get out of the country. You can go anywhere in Europe! The Czech Republic or Poland. The woman I live with now says that it is better to go to Georgia."

"Adoriana," my mother pleaded. "Don't go anywhere. Calm down. Come to us."

My parents did not share my indignation regarding Russia's invasion. My father was born in Russia. I remember visiting my Russian grandmother as a child. She had a beautiful, intricately carved cuckoo clock with spruce cone weights made from iron hanging on her living room wall. I would eagerly await the new hour and watch as the bright yellow cuckoo emerged to cheerfully announce the time.

My father fell in love with my mother, a Ukrainian woman, and they have lived in complete harmony since that day. My parents never quarreled. They sought ways to compromise. For my father, "home" was with my mother. However, he always missed his native land, especially since he has suffered all of his life from an allergy to ragweed, a plant that does not grow in the region where he's from.

There was no sense in arguing with my mother about the war over the phone. She was set in her beliefs. Just as my parents would have to release their grip on me, I would have to release my grip on them. Understandably, my mother wanted to protect me in the place she called home. What she did not realize was the place one associated with safety and peace can be blasted to oblivion in a matter of seconds.

While I was unable to phone people in Ukraine, I could phone people I knew in Russia. The only change to the system involved an automated voice of a Ukrainian operator stating, "You are calling the country's aggressor. Remind them about it," before allowing the call to go through. I attempted to phone my father's sister, who lived in Russia with my uncle and cousin. Since there were only buses heading in the direction of the east, I thought maybe they could do something to help me.

The phone rang and rang. BEEP. BEEP. BEEP. BEEP. My aunt did not pick up. I tried to phone her many times in the days that followed. She would have seen my number on the screen. She always picked up my calls before the war. At some point, it dawned on me: *She does not want to pick up the phone. She does not love me. She does not even care about me. In her mind, I am a Ukrainian pariah best left alone.* That night, I removed all of the documents from my backpack and tore the photos of my Russian relatives to shreds.

I told my mother about my aunt's silence. "Adoriana, don't judge her," she said. "Maybe they are forbidden to speak with Ukrainians. Maybe she is afraid."

"And yet I am not afraid to call her," I argued. "What difference does it make that there is a war? We are human beings. We are a family."

The rage I felt was venomous. How many times had I been asked by strangers I encountered on my journey, "How are you doing? How can we help?" And now I was in enemy territory, being sheltered and fed by a stranger while my Russian family members would not even take my calls. In contrast, I have a Ukrainian friend who moved to Krasnodar, a city in southern Russia. At the start of the invasion, he sent me a message on Instagram, "If you need help, write to me. Even though it's hard for me to realize what it's like for you, I would be glad to help."

As with Luda and Ivan, I have permanently deleted my Russian relatives from my life. "What about forgiveness?" some may ask. Ah, forgiveness—such a noble and lofty sentiment. Tell me, where can *I* find forgiveness? Is it buried in the pocket of that little bloodstained pink coat flapping in the wind? Or does it lay beneath the thousands of rotting corpses and torn limbs strewn across the streets of Mariupol? Perhaps if I dig hard enough, deep enough, I will find it like a pot of gold at the rainbow's end.

***

I contacted several of my friends who were Ukrainian soldiers stationed in Vinnytsia, a city in west-central Ukraine that was presently safe from the threat of Russian occupation. They were *in the know*, so to speak, and I trusted what they said.

"I am trapped in Nikolske," I told them. "What should I do?"

"Whatever you do," one friend replied, "*don't* go to Russia."

"Should I leave Nikolske and go to Zaporizhzhia? Or is Zaporizhzhia under Russian control as I have heard?"

My friends informed me that Zaporizhzhia had not yet been captured by the Russians. "There are fights nearby," they told me, "but Zaporizhzhia is not surrounded."

I was doubtful. Many people had told me the opposite about Zaporizhzhia. "Are you sure the situation is not like Mariupol?"

Another friend got on the line. "Listen, Adoriana," he said firmly. "You have a choice who to believe. We said that it is dangerous in Zaporizhzhia, but it is not surrounded at the moment. The decision is yours. You can stay in Nikolske for a few more days, and we will find a way to get you tomorrow or the day after tomorrow. Wait for us to come and get you—"

"But what if..." The line suddenly dropped. I could not call them back.

I told Natalia how frustrated I was to not have internet access or a mobile connection. The next day, she drove me to the outlying town of Mangush in hopes of finding a mobile connection for me to contact my friends in Vinnytsia again. Natalia also hoped to phone her son, who lived in Georgia. I was unable to connect with my friends when we got to Mangush. As we drove back, I worried that my friends had already arrived in Nikolske. What would they do when they saw I was not there? They did not have the luxury of waiting for my return. They had so much other work to do, and saving me put their lives at risk.

We returned to Nikolske and I was informed that no one had come to get me. Frustrated, I decided to take the risk and leave Nikolske on my own as soon as possible.

***

Natalia had a fluffy white Persian cat with magnetic blue eyes. Yola loved to chase cats, regardless of their elegance. For this reason, Natalia asked me to put her outside in a cage used for hunting dogs. Natalia covered the floor of the cage with straw and put a blanket on top.

The following morning, I went to retrieve Yola. She was curled up into a tight little ball. When I opened the cage door, she approached me reluctantly rather than running into my arms as usual. She had this sad look of abandonment in her eyes as if to say, *how could you leave me?* What guilt I felt! I suppose everyone gets used to a good and free life, even animals.

I walked Yola from the cage towards the house. I suddenly froze in my tracks and absorbed my surroundings. Having been underground in the dead of winter for five weeks, I was bowled over by the warmth of the sun shining like a dazzling jewel from above. It was a magical feeling, made even more magical by the sensory deprivation I had experienced while living underground.

Natalia emerged from the house. Always the attentive mother hen, she asked me if I was okay.

"Oh yes," I replied lightly. "The warm sun feels wonderful."

Natalia's face lit up. "Come see my flowers!" she said. She led me to a small garden behind her house. The delicate perennials were already breaking through the ground. "Stay with us for as long as you wish," Natalia told me. "You can help me with my garden. In the spring, everything will bloom. I will introduce you to my friend, who is a schoolteacher. She is a kind woman. You will see that Nikolske is a very friendly village."

"But how will I find work?" I asked.

Natalia gently smiled. "You are such a pretty young woman, Adoriana. We will find you a husband in Nikolske."

The mere thought of settling in a town occupied by Russia and marrying a man who likely supported the war or did not care one way or the other made my stomach sour. Just then, a series of loud explosions sounded from somewhere outside of the village. Our topic of conversation dramatically changed.

"Do you have an underground shelter?" I asked nervously.

"No," she replied. "But there is a shelter at the school if we need it."

Natalia saw how my agitation increased. I envisioned being trapped in yet another shelter with hundreds of strangers.

"Don't worry, Adoriana," Natalia soothed. "The Russian soldiers won't bomb the DPR now that they occupy it." She paused for a long time as if weighing whether to speak her next words. "Although the shelling might come from the Ukrainians, who want the land back."

Yes, today *Nikolske is safe; next month it may become a bloody war zone, just like Mariupol. No place in Ukraine is safe.*

Chapter Fifteen

On my second day in Nikolske, I went to the store and purchased some tangy Fanta lollipops and coffee from a machine. I left the store and passed a woman selling pies stacked on the hood of her parked car. My mouth watered as I examined the pies.

"How much?" I asked.

"Forty hryvnias," she answered.

The pies were ridiculously overpriced. Before the war, a loaf of bread cost between fifteen and twenty hryvnias. Nevertheless, I was willing to pay the inflated price if it meant that I could gift Natalia a fresh pie before I left town. I joined the other people waiting in line.

Russian soldiers approached. They asked the people in line, "How much does she sell them?"

No one answered. Everyone played dumb and quickly dispersed. The Russian soldiers forcibly removed the pie woman from the street.

I turned to a woman in the crowd. "What happened?" I asked. "What do they want from her? Why was she taken away?"

The woman silently scurried away. An old man stepped into the empty air. "She was removed because it's right," he said. "The military keeps order. Have you seen at what prices they sell them?"

"But where can you buy food here?" I challenged. "Maybe that woman just wanted to earn money."

The old man dismissed me with a wave of the hand and walked away. Apparently, there was nothing left to say.

Later that day, I went to the market and purchased honey, raw chicken, and fruit. The prices in the market were so much higher than in Mariupol before the invasion, and there were two price tags on every item: one in hryvnias and one in rubles. Strangely, Russian soldiers did not forbid people from shopping at the market where the food was just as overpriced as the pies the woman had tried to sell in the street.

I left the market and passed several government buildings over which the DPR had plastered pro-Russia propaganda. One poster depicting Lenin was at least fifteen meters high. I rolled my eyes at the image. *God help us,* I thought.

Russian soldiers were everywhere, all dressed in red and yellow, a nostalgic throwback to the colors of the USSR. I was thankful they could not read my thoughts, for my hatred of them was intense. I returned to Natalia's house with my gift of groceries.

Natalia was indignant. "No, Adoriana!" she exclaimed. "You must not spend the little money that you have on me."

I insisted that she accept the food. I wanted to at least do something for her. Proud people who are forced to accept charity will understand what compelled me to give back to Natalia.

***

Russian soldiers followed me whenever I walked along the streets of Nikolske. One morning, I stealthily slipped away from their radar and spoke with villagers who told me there was a man who worked in the market and transported refugees to Berdyansk for a fee. They said that Red Cross buses supposedly evacuated people from Berdyansk and drove them into central Ukraine.

I finally located this man. At that early hour, the market was empty of customers, and the two young Russian soldiers who followed me stood out like ravenous bloodhounds. The Russians had made it very clear to the people of Nikolske that transporting Ukrainians out of the village was forbidden.

"Will you drive me to Berdyansk?" I asked nervously.

He took me aside and whispered, "Look at the fruit and vegetables when you talk. Act like you shop."

I lifted a bunch of carrots and inspected them. "Please," I begged him tearfully. "I cannot stay here. You must help me. Please—"

"How much money do you have?" he interrupted gruffly.

My heart leaped with hope, I had eight thousand hryvnias (about US $271) on me. I also had three thousand hryvnias on my bank card, but that did me no good because none of the banks in the Donetsk region were operating. Perhaps I could haggle him down in price.

"Will you take a thousand hryvnias?" I asked, intent on hanging onto some of the money.

His beady eyes narrowed. "I need four thousand hryvnias, *moloda ledi*."

I furtively glanced at the two Russian soldiers. They were distracted by a grocer who had tripped and spilled a basket of potatoes onto the ground. They cruelly laughed at the humiliated woman. My eyes returned to the man.

"During peacetime," I said, "the fare for traveling from Nikolske to Berdyansk was ninety-seven hryvnias."

"This is not peacetime, is it?" he growled.

All hope evaporated. I knew he was right. No man in his right mind would risk driving a car carrying a Ukrainian refugee from Nikolske to Berdyansk unless a handsome sum of money was involved.

He hesitated for a long time. His eyes shifted from my face to the two Russian soldiers, who stood a stone's throw away. "I will take you if you find others who can also pay," he muttered under his breath. "Now buy the carrots and go away."

My mood swung yet again, and I felt hope. I happily purchased the overpriced carrots and threw a few bruised apples into the bag to seal the deal.

That afternoon, I searched around for other refugees who would join me on the trip to Berdyansk. They quickly appeared, as if by magic: a woman, her son, and another man were each willing to pitch in for the ride.

Natalia tried strongly to dissuade me. She said that I did not know this man from the market and that trusting him was very dangerous. She bluntly stated I was going to my death. She also reminded me that there was fighting in the vicinity; we could easily drive over a land mine or get shot.

I completely understood Natalia's concerns. I harbored them as well. While many agencies and individuals generously offered Ukrainian refugees assistance by transporting them to and sheltering them in countries like Poland, Romania, Moldova, Hungary, and Slovakia, predatory individuals and criminal networks were exploiting the situation. Moreover, ninety percent of the Ukrainian refugees seeking asylum were women and children, making them particularly vulnerable to traffickers and abusers.[22]

Natalia persisted, "I hope you don't plan to travel to Zaporizhzhia after you arrive in Berdyansk."

"That is exactly what I plan to do," I replied.

Her eyes widened. "Adoriana, no! Don't go, I beg you. Zaporizhzhia is in the ring of cities the Russians have already captured. You are safer here than you will be in Zaporizhzhia. I would never let my daughter go this way. It is better for you to stay here right now."

---

22. Siegfried, Kriisty. "Ukraine crisis creates new trafficking risks." *The UN Refugee Agency/USA*. 13 April 2022. https://www.unhcr.org/en-us/news/stories/2022/4/62569be24/ukraine-crisis-creates-new-trafficking-risks.html

I did not tell Natalia about my conversation with my soldier friends who told me Zaporizhzhia was not yet surrounded.

"Why not wait a while and then go to Russia?" Natalia suggested. "Once you arrive, contact my son and his wife in Georgia. Maybe you can live with them."

I adamantly shook my head. "I could easily get stuck in Russia with no way out."

"You won't go to Russia, but you will get into a car with an unfamiliar man?" Natalia argued. "At best, he will rob you and throw you into a field along the roadside!"

I stood my ground and explained to Natalia that I would be fine. After all, I had survived the horrors of Mariupol and fended off a potential rapist with a knife. I was not indomitable, but I knew how to protect myself. Natalia refused to accept my decision. She was genuinely worried about my safety like a mother hen looking out for her chicks.

I could not sleep that night. A dangerous path fraught with peril stretched out before me. At about 2 a.m., I got out of bed and went to the toilet. I saw a light in the kitchen. The air smelled of baked goods and cinnamon. I wrapped myself in the plush white bathrobe Nina had given me and entered the kitchen. Natalia stood at the counter, rolling dough on a wooden cutting board.

"Why are you not sleeping?" I asked.

Natalia's brow furrowed as her eyes remained focused on smoothing the dough with the rolling pin. "I worry about you, Adoriana. I don't know what will happen to you if you go to Zaporizhzhia, so at least I make you apple pies for the road."

My God, it was such a touching moment. We were strangers a few days before, and now she cared enough to make pies—loaded with apple slices—for me in the middle of the night. We hugged and cried in that kitchen.

"Thank you, Natalia. I will never forget your kindness," I said.

She pulled away from our embrace and stared directly into my eyes. "Adoriana, if there is a phone connection, call me. If there are any problems along the way, call me. Stick with the other passengers. They are from Ukraine, after all. When you reach your destination, write me. Do you promise?"

I rested my hand on her shoulder and returned her steady gaze. "I promise."

I remain eternally grateful to dear Natalia for the three peaceful days I spent in her home.

Chapter Sixteen

By a stroke of sheer luck, Russian soldiers did not follow me as I slipped out of Natalia's house at the break of day and snuck off to the market. I quickly located the driver. I stepped into his car, feeling like I was about to make a parachute jump from a high-flying plane. Although I was full of determination and clarity, I also had a gnawing fear something could go wrong. After all, the man who offered to drive me to Berdyansk was motivated by financial gain, not charity.

What's more, I could not trust the other passengers would serve as protection. There are a lot of vile Ukrainians who are traitors to our country. It's no surprise Russia chose to directly invade Mariupol first rather than an outlying territory. Before the invasion, residents of Mariupol were leaking information and military positions to Russia for money, knowing there would be no trial against them once the war began.

I was therefore suspicious of everyone, even my fellow Ukrainians. Adding to my concerns was that in a time of war, laws were no longer enforced. Police would not respond to calls for help, and people were killed in the blink of an eye with no repercussions. Like an arctic fox, I had to blend into the all-pervasive landscape of snow and ice and watch my back at every turn.

"Woman," the driver gruffly asked, "what's your name?"

"Adoriana," I replied.

He scrunched up his eyebrows and frowned.

"It is an uncommon name," I said.

He released a piggish grunt.

All of Natalia's warnings raced through my mind as the other passengers loaded into the car. Was I a fool to leave the safety of Natalia's home? Other thoughts simultaneously penetrated the mix. Would my military friends be waiting for me in Vinnytsia? What about my parents? Was it right for me to reject their invitation to return to their home? I saw my whole life before my eyes—the many friends who had left Mariupol behind, the fact I was now entering a vast abyss of the unknown. Looking back on it now, I see how the decision to leave Nikolske did not come from me—it came from higher powers.

The sea of Russian flags faded in the rearview mirror as we drove away from Nikolske. What relief I felt to leave. Unfortunately, there were a lot of Ukrainians in the Donbas who supported Russia. They were convinced the Russians were their brothers and sisters. Many members of the older generation watched Russian TV channels and believed everything they were told. They could not understand that Russia did not care about them as human beings but rather lusted after Ukraine's rich natural resources: the immense deposits of coal, untapped lithium, titanium, iron ore, and more coveted prizes.

In the years leading up to the invasion, Putin pursued the impending theft with remarkable cunning—throwing bait to Crimea, Donetsk, and Luhansk, redistributing the power, and planting Russians in those territories. Tightening his grip, he took advantage of the moment by establishing Russian rules in the annexed territories, sewing seeds of doubt in the heads of ordinary Ukrainians by presenting fairy-tale depictions of Russians as a "fraternal people." According to Putin, Ukrainians were like two apples growing side by side on the same branch. It was some kind of tree, I can tell you that—one rotten apple infected a healthy apple simply through physical contact.

On a positive note, there are not many fans of what I call *the Russian world* in most regions of Ukraine. I saw media footage of residents in Kherson, a city located in southern Ukraine occupied by Russian forces at the time of this writing, who bravely faced the soldiers and tanks in Freedom Square. They had no weapons, only their bare hands. They shouted at the crowd of Russian soldiers, "Get out, you bastards! Kherson is Ukraine!"[23] In response, Russian forces deployed tear gas and stun grenades to disperse the crowd.[24]

Likewise, most of us have heard about the thirteen brave Ukrainian soldiers who perished defending an island in the Black Sea from aerial and naval bombardment. When told by an officer onboard a Russian navy warship to surrender, one of the Ukrainian soldiers defiantly shouted, "Go fuck yourself!"[25]

How I admire their courage. The protestors and soldiers knew their actions could lead to death, but they did them anyway. Ukrainians are strong and unique people. We are familiar with throwing out corrupt rulers with whom we disagree. I previously referenced the mass protests that became known as the Euromaidan and the Revolution of

---

23. "Pro-Ukraine Rally Dispersed by Russians in Kherson After City Administration Forced Out." *RFE/RL Radio Free Europe/Radio Liberty.* 27 April 2022. https://www.rferl.org/a/kherson-ukrainian-rally-dispersed/31824009.html

24. Ibid.

25. Visontay, Elias. "Ukraine soldiers told Russian officer to 'go fuck yourself' before they died on island." *The Guardian.* 25 February 2022. https://www.theguardian.com/world/2022/feb/25/ukraine-soldiers-told-russians-to-go-fuck-yourself-before-black-sea-island-death Note that Ukraine enjoyed a small strategic defeat when Russian forces withdrew from Snake Island in late June 2022. See: Ilyushina, Mary, Suliman, Adela, Horton, Alex. "Russian forces withdraw from Ukraine Snake Island." *Washington Post.* 30 June 2022 https://www.washingtonpost.com/world/2022/06/30/russia-withdraw-snake-island-ukraine-war/

Dignity in 2013 and 2014, respectively. Our president at the time, Viktor Yanukovych, had strong pro-Russian leanings and rejected a pending agreement between Ukraine and the EU. He even asserted that the Great Famine of 1932-33 was not genocide.

I walked past Yanukovych's dacha at the start of the Euromaidan. The estate covers three hundred and fifty acres in the Kiev Oblast. The complex is enclosed by a five-meter-tall fence. Within that perimeter lay the trappings of a corrupt ruler's wealth, mostly funded by oligarchs who funneled billions of dollars through oil, gas, and other energy companies to Yanukovych. The dacha housed servants by the dozens, a tennis court, a golf course, hunting grounds, an ostrich farm, recreational facilities, manmade lakes, exotic flowers and trees, horse stables, a yacht ramp, and yes, even a small chapel.

When Yanukovych's corruption was uncovered, he was impeached and found guilty of treason. Many thought it was impossible to overthrow his power, but we did it. Yanukovych was exiled to Russia.[26] His lavish dacha has been made into a museum, complete with all of the luxury cars owned by the once powerful man.

I was surprised to see there was almost no destruction along the roadway from Nikolske to Berdyansk. We saw only a few burnt-out cars. Nikolske, Melitopol, and Mangush had surrendered without a fight. We passed several Russian checkpoints on the 133.6-kilometer drive to Berdyansk. Drawn-out lines of cars waited at the checkpoints. The soldiers took a long time examining each entrant and searching through their data, thus delaying our trip by many hours.

---

26. Roth, Andrew. "Ukraine's ex-President Viktor Yanukovych found guilty of treason." *The Guardian*. 25 January 2019. https://www.theguardian.com/world/2019/jan/25/ukraine-ex-president-viktor-yanukovych-found-guilty-of-treason

My pulse quickened as the Russians ordered us to get out of the car and present our papers and mobile phones. Surrendering my cell phone would equate to losing my line of communication with the free world. For that reason, I had previously deleted all of my contacts and social media, along with photos I had taken of the carnage in Mariupol, having heard through the grapevine that Russian soldiers wanted to confiscate any record of their crimes.

It felt like I was walking past rabid animals as I moved forward in the queue. I behaved calmly. I had nothing to hide but that did not matter. Russian soldiers were in search of any form of evidence, fabricated or real, that could land my ass in a Russian prison. I tried not to roll my eyes when the soldiers inspected our arms and legs for tattoos depicting swastikas and the like. *Are you crazy?* I wanted to shout. *Do you believe that bullshit?*

Apparently, the DPR soldiers did believe the bullshit. They sometimes referenced a neo-Nazi unit of Ukraine's National Guard based in Mariupol as proof that all Ukrainians were neo-Nazis. In 2010, the first Azov commander, Andriy Biletsky, announced his aspiration to "lead the white races of the world in a final crusade."[27]

Nevertheless, white supremacy is more marginal in Ukraine than in Russia and, arguably, in many NATO countries, including America. In 2014, the founder of the homophobic and antisemitic Right Sector, Dmytro Yarosh, ran for president and garnered less than one percent of the vote. Similarly, in 2019, the Right Sector and other far-right groups sought to fill Ukraine's parliament. They failed to win a single seat. That same year, we elected Volodymyr Zelensky, "a Russian-speaking Jew whose great-grandparents had died in the Holocaust," by a landslide.[28]

---

27. Mogelson, Luke. "Letter from Ukraine, The Wound Dressers." *New Yorker.* 9 May 2022. p. 55

28. Ibid

That's not to say that the white supremacists did not continue to rear their ugly heads from time to time. There were showdowns at football matches, and petty white supremacist hooligans picked fights in the streets. They were little more than a criminal nuisance, and they were dealt with accordingly by Ukrainian law enforcement.

A Russian soldier presently seized the phone of a Ukrainian man standing behind me in the queue. The man made no secret of voicing his resentment. "I need my phone!" he said angrily, to which the Russian soldier calmly replied, "Shut up and get on the bus."

A chestnut-haired woman in her early twenties waited ahead of me in the line. A Russian soldier scrolled through the photos on the young woman's cell phone. Any random image could result in arrest. For example, a photo of a house was cause for suspicion. Although the image was harmless, the Russian soldiers could say it revealed their military positions to snipers. Additionally, a simple photo of the Ukrainian flag or a bandura (a traditional Ukrainian instrument) could indicate allegiance to the Ukrainian state and subject one to aggressive interrogation.

The soldier saw something on the young woman's phone that caused him to remove her from the group and escort her into a building. She may have been arrested and sent to prison, or she may have been transported back to a filtration camp in Russian-occupied territory. I sincerely hoped the woman's process would not entail beating and torturing her. One Russian soldier working at a makeshift filtration center was heard saying, "I killed ten, and didn't count further."[29] In the end, I have no way of knowing what happened to the young woman. Like so many Ukrainians who have fallen

---

29. Kottasova, Ivana, and Oleksandra, Ochman. "Ukrainians must endure a brutal 'filtration' process to escape Russian-held territory. Here's what that means" *CNN.* 23 May 2022. https://www.cnn.com/2022/05/23/europe/russia-ukraine-filtration-camps-intl-cmd/index.html

prey to Russian aggression, her future whereabouts have been erased from history, just like the photos on her phone.

Photos

Adoriana greets the Statue of Liberty

*Adoriana in bomb-shelter (face blurred
to protect the author's identity)*

Putin's Punch

Yola on Mountain, Czech Republic

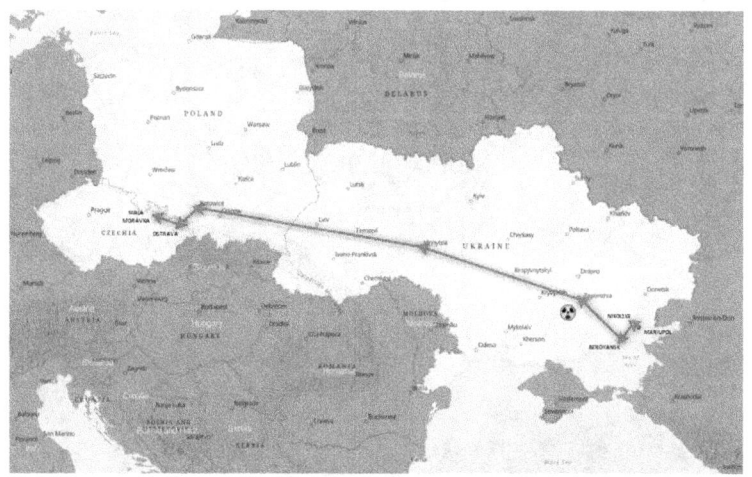

Adoriana's Escape Route

Chapter Seventeen

We arrived safely in Berdyansk. Situated on the northern coast of the Sea of Azov, the seaport city boasts sandy beaches, health resorts, mud baths, and other tourist attractions. There are also profitable chemical and petroleum-refining industries on the outskirts of Berdyansk. There was little to do in the coastal city in the autumn and winter. However, in summer, the streets and beaches exploded with life. Ukrainians have an expression for crowded areas: "there is no place for a needle to fall." There was also no place to park your body on a towel at the beach.

Needless to say, my time in Berdyansk was far from a vacation. Unlike Mariupol, the weather was dry and relatively warm—about 6°C. As in Nikolske, Russian flags, pro-Russian posters, billboards, and brush-stroked white *Z*s were everywhere. I was desperate to get out of Dodge, as Americans would say. The sooner, the better.

I used to travel to Berdyansk on business before the war. During those trips, I finished my work as quickly as possible so I could purchase a cup of delicious coffee from a streetside café and walk along the embankment to feed the seagulls. In winter, the city was calming and atmospheric. I would stroll along the central roadway leading to the Azov Sea and think about my parents. Their love story always struck a chord with me. My Ukrainian mother came to Berdyansk in the late 1970s to study at an art institute. My

Russian father traveled there on business, selling parts and materials to the many machine factories in the city.

According to my mother, she and a friend left the art institute one evening and sat down to rest on a bench by the shore. My father and his friend caught sight of the pair and decided to get acquainted with them, although both men had eyes for my mother. Years later, I would survey the embankment, wondering on which rusted old bench my mother and her friend sat when she first met my father. Was it close to the gold-domed alcove? Or near the lookout where the funny-looking statue of *The Envious Toad* now stands?

According to my father, my young mother was very cute, a modest girl, and a little timid. Faded Polaroid photos reveal my mother was not just cute, she was a true Ukrainian beauty—long silky blonde hair, high cheekbones lifting to powder blue eyes, and a very slender figure boasting wide, childbearing hips that her future daughters would one day inherit and curse.

My mother did not accept the invitation to go out with either of the good-looking Russian men. Undeterred, the next day, my father and his friend visited the boarding house where my mother and her friend lived and they all went for a walk. My father was intent on winning my mother's heart. Though she enjoyed my father's company, her somewhat aloof response only increased my father's infatuation.

Thereafter, my mother frequently avoided the two ardent Russian suitors and would only walk with them if her friend came along. During their walks, my father and his friend tried to impress my mother with their accomplishments. My mother didn't seem to care that much. She was equally unaffected by my father's good looks—his tall, muscular stature, his confident smile, and a strong, angular face topped by thick waves of jet-black hair.

My dad was flummoxed. Though shy, my mother was fiercely independent. He did not know how to win her heart.

She was focused on her studies and in no hurry to start a relationship. He extended his business trip into autumn. When his friend returned to Russia, my father seized the opportunity to have time alone with my mother. He knew when she left the boarding house to go to her classes. One morning, he waited beneath the stairway, hiding a bouquet of red roses in his coat. As she approached the landing, my father emerged with the flowers and asked, "Can you be with me, Sveta? I want to marry you!"

My mother was delighted with the romantic gesture. She told my father that she would consider his proposal, evasively adding that she was leaving Berdyansk in a few days to be with her parents. If my father managed to find her, then maybe she would agree to marry him.

It was quite difficult for my father to locate my elusive mother, but he was madly in love and so he rose to the challenge. There were no smartphones, no internet. He tried to find her address for a long time. My mother's friend eventually told my father where my mother's parents lived. My father went directly to their house and asked my mother's parents for her hand in marriage.

My grandfather immediately liked my dad because he presented as a hardworking and purposeful man who was very intelligent and exceptionally well-mannered. Fortunately, there was a happy ending for my father's business associate as well. He attended my parents' wedding and met a young woman at the ceremony whom he ended up marrying.

I used to beg my parents to return to Berdyansk for a second honeymoon. My siblings and I often offered to pay for the trip. My parents always had an excuse. "That's the past," they would say, "we're different now."

I presently wandered the streets of Berdyansk with the people I had traveled with from Nikolske. Everything about the city that once invoked positive feelings now caused depression. We were told Red Cross evacuation buses waited for refugees at a local sports complex. We went to the complex where a crowd of people stood outside. No one knew for sure if the buses were still going to the complex. Some said the Russians were not allowing any buses to leave the city. I was crestfallen. We had no mobile connection, and no information was provided regarding if and when the buses would show up.

"I heard the Red Cross buses stop behind the ring on the road leading to the village of Lunacharsky," one man said.

"No!" an irritated woman insisted. "They only come here!"

The two began to argue about it. I turned to leave and a guy, who later introduced himself as Stepan, asked me, "They didn't say where the buses stop?"

"Nobody seems to know," I replied. "But we probably won't be leaving today. Do you know where people spend the night here?"

"I heard there is a school nearby," he answered. "Let's ask him."

We walked to another guy who possessed an air of confidence but like everyone else, he was clueless. "Can I look for a place with you guys?" he asked.

His name was Artem, and he looked decent enough. Stepan and I agreed, and our motley crew was formed. I instinctively sensed the two men were not only harmless but also willing to protect me if required. None of us knew what would happen tomorrow or what awaited us in general, but somehow being together gave us a sense of strength.

We aimlessly wandered the city streets. Curfew approached. The sky grew dark. A familiar panic rose inside me when we were erroneously informed there were no refugee shelters. We finally located a school, where we spent the night in a gym. There were no beds, only piles of clothing strewn across the concrete floor. Later that night, I walked down a pitch-black hallway and filled a plastic bottle with water from the fountain. I returned to the dark gym where Stepan and Artem sat eating cookies beside a stack of children's coats.

"Want one?" Stepan asked.

I sat down and took a cookie. As we ate, Stepan told me he had a wife and child. In the early days of the war, he ran out into the street and tried to flag down a car to transport his family out of Ukraine. After several unproductive hours, a church minibus slowed to the side of the road. The driver told Stepan that he could transport his wife and child out of Ukraine, but because Stepan was of draft age, the driver could not transport him. He told Stepan that he was sorry, but he didn't want to get in trouble.

"That's too bad," I said. "Many men managed to leave the country in the early days, legally or not."

He nodded. "The worst part was not knowing who those people were and where they would take my wife and son. There was no connection with them for a month. I was a wreck." His voice softened. "One day, my wife phoned me and said that they were safe in the Czech Republic. They were doing very well." Stepan suddenly burst into tears, emitting loud, uncontrollable sobs.

Artem attempted to dilute the situation by making silly jokes. Stepan wiped his face and weakly smiled. I reached into my backpack and retrieved Yola's tennis ball, trying, like Artem, to distract Stepan from the sorrow that weighed on him.

"Here, girl, go fetch!" I tossed the ball across the gym. Yola used to love to play fetch, but after weeks of not being allowed to walk further than two meters away from me, she lay at my feet and stared vacantly at the ball. *How sad,* I thought, *she has lost the habit of running.*

Stepan and Artem lay down to sleep. I walked to one of the enormous windows and stared out at the constellations. "Guys, are we going to leave tomorrow?" I asked. "Will the buses arrive?"

"Yes, of course," Stepan reassured me. "A lot of people have already left on Red Cross buses. Go to sleep. We'll walk to the sports complex first thing tomorrow and if the buses aren't there, we'll go towards the village of Lunacharsky and find that field."

Moments later, a man caught a radio wave and heard that thirty Red Cross buses would arrive at the open field on the outskirts of the city first thing in the morning. He announced the news, and everyone cheered.

I sat down on the cold concrete floor and hugged Yola to my chest. "Don't worry, *moya vyshen'ka*," I murmured softly. "We'll catch the bus in the morning. Everything is fine…"

Chapter Eighteen

The following day, I awoke at dawn, stuffed my backpack with dog food, bottled water, and the last slices of Natalia's apple pie, and walked twenty minutes to a bus stop, where I waited with Stepan and Artem for a city bus to take us to an outlying field located two kilometers away.

My back ached from the pack's heavy weight as I trudged from the bus stop to the field. I was nauseous from involuntary fasting. The school where I was staying served one meal to the refugees each day, and it was lunch. To catch the morning bus to Zaporizhzhia, I had to forego that one free meal and fight back the queasiness. True, half of Natalia's pie remained in my pack, but I needed to ration it over the course of the next few days. I also suffered headaches, fevers, and bouts of acute fatigue. At the age of thirty-one, I felt like an old woman—weak and profoundly depressed.

I lifted my eyes to the overcast sky. Oddly, no birds flew overhead. At this time of year, curlew sandpipers migrate to breeding grounds in the Russian tundra, and magpies, crows, tits, and sparrows gradually emerge from their winter nests. *Had the invasion driven the birds away?* I wondered. *Yes, this war will end sooner or later, but the consequences for nature will take much longer to play out.*

I thought about the environmental destruction Putin's war had brought to Ukraine. Soldiers dug trenches near

Chernobyl, inadvertently unleashing radiation buried in the ground. Tanks crushed vegetation. Oil depots, gas lines, and chemical plants were bombed and spewed toxic gases into the air. Ukrainians and Europeans alike worried it was just a matter of time before one or more of the country's fifteen nuclear reactors would suffer damage, resulting in a catastrophe like Chernobyl in 1986.[30] Not for the first time and certainly not for the last, I cursed Putin and his reckless brigades.

In early April, the temperatures hovered below 10°C, and a frigid wind ripped through the field. About a thousand refugees were waiting with me in that field. The first day was the easiest because we truly believed the buses would arrive at any moment. The men I was with played with Yola in the field. We stood there until 4 p.m. No buses arrived. I returned to the bus stop with Yola that evening, my heart heavy with dismay. The shops in town closed at 3 p.m. each afternoon. Even if they were still open, I would not have found much food in them. The shelves were nearly bare and the few items that remained were outdated and exorbitantly overpriced.

We returned to the school we had slept in the night before. The woman at the entrance refused to allow us inside. I showed her our passports and reminded her that our information was listed in the notebook where she kept track of guests.

"Please," I begged. "You let us stay here last night."

She shot me an icy grin. "All of the cots are full," she stated. "You shouldn't have shown up so late."

My eyes widened. "We were waiting for the Red Cross buses! What choice did we have?"

She smirked. "Find somewhere else to sleep."

---

30. Anthes, Emily. "A 'Silent Victim': How Nature Becomes a Casualty of War." *New York Times*. 13 April 2022. https://www.nytimes.com/2022/04/13/science/war-environmental-impact-ukraine.html

I completely lost my shit. "No! I will spend the night on these steps!" I screamed.

At this, she threw down the gauntlet. "You will *not* stay on the steps!" she ordered. "Now get out of here!"

I cursed her with all of the obscenities I knew. Stepan intervened. "Adoriana, calm down. We'll find somewhere to sleep. Don't humiliate yourself in front of her. Don't be like her."

I stormed off, my eyes erupting in a sea of tears. The sun had lowered. A strong wind blew in the street. My poor health made it impossible to endure the cold. I crumpled against the nearest bench. Stepan and Artem sat beside me as Yola placed her mournful face on my knees.

I gathered whatever strength I had left and rose from the bench. "We're wasting our time sitting here," I said. "Let's go. Night is coming."

Our phones had run out of power. The streets quickly emptied with the approach of curfew and there was no one to ask for help. We walked for miles and finally found another school. Fearing I would experience another meltdown, Stepan left me standing with Artem and went inside to see if there were any vacancies.

He then emerged from the side entrance and waved at me and Artem. "Guys, come in! There are places for us to sleep!"

I entered the lobby and turned to the man in charge. "Where do we go?"

"The basement," he replied absently.

I exploded with hysterical laughter. "The basement!" I bellowed as though it were the funniest thing I ever heard. The man must have thought I was a lunatic.

There was an outlet in the back corner of the basement. We waited in line to charge our phones. Instead of beds, mattresses lay over desks, or people pushed chairs together to avoid the cold concrete floor. It was not until we threw our backpacks down that we realized we had not eaten since earlier that morning when I tossed self-discipline and self-interest to the wind, sharing with Stepan and Artem what remained of Natalia's apple pie.

"Guys, we need to find out if there is food here," I said.

"I already talked to someone about it," Artem said. "We need to give them our passport data and they will serve us lunch at noon tomorrow."

"A lot of good that will do us," I muttered. "We have to get on the city bus and head for the field first thing in the morning. Maybe I can find an open supermarket."

"Don't be so naïve," Stepan said. "Nothing is open."

I groaned. "Tell me there are showers...."

Stepan shook his head. "No showers."

I turned to Artem. "Will you take a walk with me?" The last thing I wanted to do was sit in a crowded basement.

Artem nodded. Stepan frowned. "It's past curfew. Don't you have enough problems, Adoriana? You want to make things worse by going outside?"

I defiantly threw on my coat and walked to the door. Artem followed after me. Outside, the wind was as strong and icy as it had been in Mariupol during the invasion. The streets resembled the set of a *Twilight Zone* episode. No people. No cars. Only an unnatural silence magnified by the wind. Words cannot convey the dejection I felt. The people of Berdyansk were safely stowed away in the surrounding apartments while fellow Ukrainians fleeing war zones were forced to sleep underground without food.

The next morning, we located a church with an outdoor booth offering free breakfasts to refugees. The meal comprised three tablespoons of wheat porridge, a slice of bread, and tea in which something like jam floated. We were so delighted with this terrible stew. We sat on a street bench and woofed it down.

My gaze turned to the church. "Can you believe that I have never been inside a church?" I remarked, almost wistfully. "Which one of you wants to go inside with me?"

"No," Stepan grunted.

"No," Artem concurred.

Seeing my disappointment, Stepan stood up and faced me on the bench. "It's clear we are here for a reason," he said. "Let's go inside."

I smiled. "We'll see how it is and pray for the buses and ourselves."

Artem snorted. "I'm not going to that church. It probably stinks of incense."

Stepan and I left Artem on the bench and entered the church. It was beautiful inside. A spacious hall came to life with tall paintings and religious icons hovering above tables that held burning candles.

"Do you know any prayers?" I asked Stepan.

"You must be joking," he said.

I walked to an old granny sitting in a back pew. "Grandma," I whispered. "We want to pray some special prayers. Can you help us? We don't know how to do it."

"Just say everything that worries you and ask God to help," she replied sweetly. "That's all you need to do. But first, you must purchase a church candle."

Prayer won't work without a candle, I thought. I purchased a candle and lit it on the table.

Granny's heels came clomping down the aisle. "That's not where you put the candle to rest," she huffed with indignation. "If you buy the candle from that table, you put it to rest on the table over there." She pointed to another table in the corner of the church where a clearer connection to God existed.

I walked past the altar and obediently placed the candle on the correct table. I silently but ardently prayed: *God, please help me, please help my friends, protect our soldiers, save Ukraine...*

Chapter Nineteen

For three more days, we awoke at dawn, traveled to the field, and stood with the crowd of refugees waiting for the Red Cross buses to arrive. On my first day in the field, I overheard a conversation between a man and a woman in their late twenties. It was evident they were strangers to one another. On the second day, I spotted the couple together. They were smiling and easily conversing. On the third day, I saw that the two had romantically bonded. They now held hands. The starry-eyed man bashfully stole little kisses from the woman when he thought no one was looking. It was nice to see love blossoming amid so much hardship.

The buses never came. Each evening, I returned to the school less hopeful than before. Early one evening, I took Yola for a walk along the school grounds. I considered returning to Natalia in Nikolske but the price was too high. I had to keep moving forward.

A woman emerged from a nearby house with her poodle in tow. She was neatly dressed, so obviously not a refugee. In contrast, my appearance was simply terrible. Her dog saw Yola and happily headed in our direction. As Yola and the woman's poodle sniffed tails and hopped about, we struck up a conversation.

"Is everything okay with you?" she asked.

"No," I replied honestly. "I'm from Mariupol. I've been stuck here for several days. There's no shower in the school basement and we don't eat normally."

She gasped. "My God…. Let's go to my house. You can take a shower and eat."

In peacetime, it would never have occurred to me to take a shower in a stranger's house, but as the saying goes, desperate times called for desperate measures.

"Excuse me," I said. "But I cannot come to your house alone. I'm with two guys I met here. They are also refugees and have not taken a shower for a long time either."

Her smile lowered. Her face darkened with worry.

"Don't worry," I added quickly. "They are ordinary, good guys."

She relaxed. "Well, of course, call them."

I ran back to the basement and phoned Stepan and Artem. Stepan was very shy and refused to go to the woman's apartment; Artem agreed to join me.

The woman lived with her mother. They were wonderful, sincere people. Artem and I sat at their kitchen table, and we all conversed as though we had known each other for years. It was hours past curfew when we left the apartment. The woman gave us food for our journey, and we exchanged phone numbers. Artem and I walked back to the school, clean and well-fed. We laughed about how we would make fun of Stepan for not taking advantage of a free shower and food. It appears the joke was on us, however. Back at the school, the basement was empty of refugees. A note from Stepan sat on the mattress where I slept.

ADORIANA, BUSES ARRIVED FOR EVACUATION. FIND VOLUNTEERS TO BRING YOU TO THE FIELD.

The written words were like cold water poured all over me. I ran upstairs to the hallways, shouting for volunteers to take me to the field but night had fallen and no one was around. A young woman emerged from the shadows.

"Hush," she said, placing her finger to her lips. "Don't make so much noise. Where have you been?"

I explained the situation. "How could the buses leave after curfew?" I asked tearfully.

She shrugged. "I don't know, but they left about a half hour ago."

I was in shock. I dropped to my knees and sobbed hysterically. *I don't want to live anymore*, I thought. *I have no more strength left to fight. Will there ever be an end to these torments?*

I lambasted myself for refusing to stay at an abandoned gas station close to the ring. Refugees slept there so they could walk to the field at dawn each day. It was almost like sleeping in the street as there were no windows or doors for protection from the elements. *Damn it, Adoriana!* I silently cursed. *Why didn't you stay at the gas station? None of this would be happening if you made a different choice!*

Artem stood silently at my side. Out of nowhere, a scary-looking man entered the hallway. He looked like an escaped convict, with menacing eyes and dark facial stubble.

"How can I help you so that you don't cry?" he asked me.

I stared up at him in disbelief.

"How can I help you?" he repeated.

"I can't leave the city," I replied. "But I can't stay here either. I don't have a home."

He reached into his pocket and handed me a fat wad of twenty-dollar bills. "You want money? Here, take it."

"I don't need money. I just need to get to Zaporizhzhia."

"Don't worry," he said. "I will take care of everything."

Looking back, it all seems like a fantasy. I can assure you, it happened. So many people serendipitously came to me throughout my journey, as if appearing from nothing—each one serving as a stepping stone to place my foot and move across turbulent waters.

"Where are you staying now?" the man asked.

"I sleep in the basement."

"Tomorrow I will arrange for you to be taken out of the city," he said.

We parted ways, agreeing to meet on the street outside the school the next morning. I went down to the basement where Artem sat on a desk eating potato chips.

"Should I trust that man?" I asked him. "What are you planning to do?"

He shrugged haplessly. "There's nothing I can do except go to the field again tomorrow and hope more buses arrive. Maybe a miracle will happen."

I did not sleep that night. I tossed and turned on the row of desks and debated my options. I considered leaving the school and walking to another city in the dark of the night. The mere thought of it induced a panic attack. I rose from the floor and walked outside with Yola to recover. *Take deep breaths, Adoriana. Deep breath in, deep breath out.* I pulled out my phone and suddenly there was a mobile connection. I immediately started looking for information about the Red Cross buses that had arrived at the school and discovered they had arrived at the field that night and would depart for Zaporizhzhia at seven the next morning.

I rushed back to the basement and shook Artem awake. "I found information on the internet," I said. "It says the buses will be waiting in the field in the morning. It makes no sense. How can they be there in the morning when they already left? What should I do, Artem? Should I wait for the man who promised to help me, or go with you on the city bus to the field and risk missing the departure?"

"What do you want to do?" he asked.

"I have no clue. I'm at a dead end. Should I trust the internet, or wait for that man to help me? He didn't exactly inspire confidence." I knew that one wrong choice could lead to even greater sorrow.

We agreed that Artem would take the city bus to the ring in the morning, and I would stay behind to wait for the man.

If the buses were at the field, Artem promised to phone me, and I would have to figure out a way to get to the field. If the buses did not arrive, I would go with the man.

The next morning, I went outside with Yola earlier than the agreed-upon time to meet the man.

He approached from an alleyway. "Why are you here so early?"

I told him I saw a message on the internet that the Red Cross buses had arrived, but I couldn't confirm the veracity of the message and I couldn't get through to the guys I was with because I had lost my mobile connection.

"That can't be," he said. "I saw the buses leave the school yesterday. Go back to the basement. I'll come for you in about an hour."

Tears filled my eyes. I was frightened by the unknown. I was also frightened of this man.

"Just don't start crying," he told me. "We will leave soon."

"What if these messages on the internet are true?" I asked.

He sighed. "Well, if it is easier for you, we'll go to this ring that you speak of and if there are no buses there, then we will return to the city, and you will leave with my people."

What kind of people is he talking about? I wondered nervously. *Members of his family? Criminals?*

The man showed back up an hour later and I got into his car. We drove in the direction of the ring. As we approached the checkpoint, my heart skipped a beat. I could not believe my eyes. Hordes of Red Cross buses lined the horizon. Russian soldiers would not allow us to drive past the checkpoint. I flung open the car door and without so much as a thank you to the man who had either helped me or planned to traffic me, I jumped out and ran full speed past a row of Russians with machine guns.

People shouted from the bus, "Don't run so, we're not leaving yet!"

My heart nearly burst with happiness. I was one step closer to freedom. *I'm glad the granny told me to put the candle on the correct table,* I mused.

Chapter Twenty

I met people in the field who had sheltered with me in the school basements. They told me they boarded the buses the night before and were taken to a nearby village because the Russian soldiers would not allow the buses to stay in the field during curfew. They had spent the night in the village and the buses transported them back to the field for the last remaining refugees to board first thing that morning.

As I boarded the bus with Yola strapped to my side, a Russian soldier shouted, "What are you doing with a dog? It takes space that could be used for a woman and child!"

I feared he would throw both of us off the bus and I would be stranded once again. I pretended I did not hear him. Thankfully, the soldier moved on to other activities and left us alone.

As I walked down the aisle, a woman glared at Yola from her seat. "Why are you bringing that filthy sausage on the bus?" she asked. I silently cursed her and found an empty seat. I settled into it with Yola hiding beneath my legs. Once every seat was filled, the bus jerked into motion, and off we went.

It was one hell of a road. In peacetime, the journey from Berdyansk to Zaporizhzhia took three hours. In our present circumstances, the trip took over ten hours. We passed through at least eight Russian checkpoints. We had to wait on the bus until we were given permission by the soldiers to step outside, where our bodies were searched and our documents inspected. At one of the checkpoints, a woman stepped off the bus with her child, who needed to go to the bathroom.

"Quickly get in!" a Russian soldier shouted angrily. The woman grabbed her child and rushed back onto the bus. The Russian soldier entered the bus and yelled at all of us, "If someone else leaves this bus without permission, we will shoot you all! The same will happen to those I see with phones in their hands. I see one phone, you all get shot!"

The fire in that soldier's eyes and the hatred in his voice sent a torrent of terror through the bus. The woman sat in the seat beside me with her little boy perched on her lap. "I have to go, Mama," he whimpered.

I reached into my backpack and handed her one of the plastic bags I used for Yola. The bus jerked into motion and the little boy defecated while we were driving. The stench was unbearable. It was a cold and windy day. The passengers opened all the windows, and the rickety vehicle became a freezer on wheels.

My empty stomach lurched as the bus left the road and crossed fields where fighting had recently taken place. The small vehicles were not designed to travel over uneven turf. They swayed from side to side, threatening to roll over at any second. We weren't allowed to drive with headlights on, so we were driving with flashing emergency lights. I still had a temperature from whatever virus I had been fighting since I left the shelter. I moaned with discomfort. At times, I came close to vomiting. I restrained the urge. The last thing I wanted was to add to the malodor surrounding us.

The land teemed with unexploded shells and mines. I feebly reassured myself that my position in the middle column of the bus would provide some form of protection if we drove over a mine. I stared out the window as the vehicle's flashing emergency lights revealed mountains of burnt and wrecked tanks and equipment. Any one of the Red

Cross buses could have exploded during the trip through those fields, adding to the carnage and wreckage.

I once again thought about the impact the war was having on wheat production. With its fertile black soil and close access to international seaports, Ukraine is known as the breadbasket of Europe. According to the *New York Times*, "Russia and Ukraine together supply more than a quarter of the world's wheat and coming disruptions could fuel higher food prices and social unrest."[31] There would be no wheat planted or harvested in the fields over which we traveled for a long time to come. By the summer of 2022, the cost of the damage to Ukraine's agricultural industry would rise to $4.3 billion.[32]

The buses finally arrived in Zaporizhzhia, a city in southeastern Ukraine located on the banks of the Dnieper River. As with many Ukrainian cities, Zaporizhzhia is a major manufacturer of steel, aluminum, automobiles, and other heavy industrial goods. The city also contains three nuclear power plants. The Zaporizhzhia Nuclear Power Plant is the largest nuclear power station in Europe. Russian forces occupied the plant complex shortly after the invasion of Mariupol while Ukrainian workers were forced to keep it running. One month earlier, on March 3, 2022, Russian forces recklessly caused a fire near the plant, threatening a potential nuclear meltdown. Fortunately, firefighters were able to vanquish the flames and avoid a greater tragedy.[33]

31. Swanson, Ana. "Ukraine Invasion Threatens Global Wheat Supply." *New York Times.* 23 March 2022. https://www.nytimes.com/2022/02/24/business/ukraine-russia-wheat-prices.html

32. Latzke, Jennifer, M. "The agricultural cost of Russia's war in Ukraine" *American Agriculturalist.* 30 June 2022. https://www.farmprogress.com/wheat/agricultural-cost-russias-war-ukraine

33. Thomas, Peter. "Ukraine officials say fire at nuclear power plant erupted outside perimeter." *Reuters.* 3 March 2022. https://www.reuters.com/world/europe/ukraine-officials-say-fire-nuclear-power-plant-erupted-outside-perimeter-2022-03-04/

In the months to come, the threat of hydrogen leakage and the release of radioactive substances from the plant would threaten residents in the vicinity. Iodide pills were handed out to everyone. Making matters worse, the risk of future fires or a complete meltdown set all of Europe on edge. In early September, satellite images revealed a gaping hole in the roof of the nuclear plant. It's only a matter of time before Russia's reckless and inhumane decision to station troops at the plant and fire missiles from the surrounding grounds results in tragedy.

Chapter Twenty-One

We were all eager to step off the bus in Zaporizhzhia, stretch our legs, and breathe fresh air. As we stood and gathered our scant baggage, the bus driver instructed us to sit back down and wait for Ukrainian reporters to take photos. It was sheer absurdity. The passengers on the bus went ballistic. The trip had been hellish, and their patience had run dry. Some kicked at the doors and broke the windows. They cursed and yelled and shoved one another down the narrow aisle. *I survived Mariupol only to get killed by Ukrainians on this bus,* I thought.

A woman screamed, "Let me out of this bus!" She pointed her finger at me. "And you, stop coughing in my direction!"

I sprayed all of the rage bottled up inside of me on that woman. "Have you tried to close your filthy mouth?" I shouted. "I feel terrible! I can hardly stand on my feet! I can't help but cough, I am sick!"

Yola huddled under the seat, her ears flattened and her eyes wide with terror. The little boy sitting on his mother's lap sobbed loudly. Ukrainian volunteers eventually entered the bus and wrote down all of our data. Hours later, we were allowed to get off the bus. It was 3 a.m. I ignored the reporters shouting questions at us and located a volunteer. I handed him my passport and anxiously told him that I needed to go to Vinnytsia right away.

"Calm down," he said. "Today you are not going anywhere. Go inside that shopping center to get some supplies."

I entered a store that had been converted into a refugee center. I asked the woman at the counter where I could wash and go to the toilet. She pointed in the direction of the public restrooms and handed me a package containing a toothbrush, toothpaste, socks, and underpants. I cherished those simple gifts.

The volunteers called for everyone to return to the bus. They told us that we would travel to a school where we could stay the night. It was yet another long trip in pitch-black darkness. Roadblocks were everywhere. Unlike Mariupol. Zaporizhzhia was covered in anti-tank hedgehogs and fortifications made with enormous sandbags. The bus finally stopped on a side street and the volunteers lit the path for us with flashlights. When we arrived at the school, we were offered tea, coffee, sandwiches, pies, and fruit, but none of us had an appetite.

I put a pie into my backpack and collapsed onto one of the little cots that lined the room. The beds were so tiny that grown men laid down with their legs hanging off the mattresses. We all slept like the dead for two hours.

At seven, volunteers woke us and offered us food. We were still too exhausted to eat. We were then taken to a bus station where we could sign up for a free train to Lviv, a city in western Ukraine located about sixty kilometers from the Polish border.

My phone suddenly lit up with messages from friends who had been unable to reach me since the start of the invasion.

ADORIANA, WHERE ARE YOU? ADORIANA,
ARE YOU ALL RIGHT? ADORIANA, WE ARE SO
WORRIED, PLEASE CALL US RIGHT AWAY!

The messages were distinctly different from those I received from members of my family in recent weeks. No one in my family ever told me they were worried about me. My mother simply instructed me to write or phone my aunt in Russia and stay put in a safe shelter. She stated innocently:

EVERYTHING WILL SOON PASS. BE PATIENT, MY DEAR.
DON'T GO ANYWHERE. CALM DOWN. WAIT FOR THE
OFFICIAL EVACUATION. WE HEARD ON THE RADIO
THAT THE MINISTER OF GREECE WILL SOON ARRIVE
IN UKRAINE. HE WILL HELP WITH NEGOTIATIONS.

My mother was well-intentioned but misguided. It was a hard dose of reality to accept. I could not trust her counsel—only I could save myself.

I began to text everyone back while sporadically checking media outlets for information about the invasion. My childhood friend, Katya, moved to Poland several years ago. She presently works as a manager for a Polish company. I saw she had left three voicemail messages. She had visited an online site listing the names of civilians who had recently left Mariupol and saw my name on the list. We were no longer close. Katya had phoned me out of curiosity.

"Katya, how are your mother and sister?" I asked. "Are they still in Mariupol?"

Katya's voice broke with sorrow. "They are both dead, Adoriana. Their apartment building was bombed."

I thought of Katya's sweet mother, the way she always welcomed me into her home and served us cups of uzvar, and her sister, so vivacious and equally kind. I couldn't understand how this could happen in a cultured country like Ukraine. What a loss. What a tragic, *senseless* loss.

Katya's mother and sister lived close to the historic part of the city. "Why didn't they hide in the Drama Theater?" I asked.

"Haven't you heard? The Drama Theater was bombed. Hundreds of civilians were killed in the attack."

I pressed my eyes shut and tried to process the horrific news. How easily I could have been killed at the Drama Theater. I had chosen to stay beneath the auto parts store rather than run to the seemingly impenetrable Drama Theater only because the theater was located in a section of the city where the Russians were concentrating their efforts. Not that the shelter beneath the store was any safer, but that random decision had saved my life. The final death count at the Drama Theater would eventually rise to six hundred— most of them women and children.

"No place was safe in Mariupol," she lamented.

Don't I know it. I ended the call with Katya and phoned a former co-worker, Olha. We had a good relationship in the workplace, but I did not consider her to be a close friend. I was therefore surprised to see that she had sent me so many texts and voicemails in recent weeks, desperately inquiring about my status.

Now she and I began to communicate in a completely different way. I learned from our phone conversation that she was not the ordinary woman I had assumed her to be. For the first time, Olha told me that her husband worked for the SBU—Ukraine's Secret Service. When I went missing during the invasion, Olha frequently phoned my parents to see if they had heard from me. She had also been looking for people to take me out of Mariupol. Her concern for my welfare moved me to tears. As with so many people during the war, Olha's true colors were revealed.

After returning every one of the messages, I turned my gaze to the long queue of refugees waiting for their free train tickets to Lviv. I was too tired and sick to stand in line with them, let alone take the train to Lviv, which required transferring to another train in Przemyśl, Poland. What I needed more than anything was the support of the soldier friends I had contacted at Natalia's house. I was kind to them in the past. They would sometimes visit my apartment in Mariupol. I would make them borscht for dinner and a special pie for dessert. We would talk and laugh for hours. I knew I could trust those men.

I used a rideshare app to locate a driver who could take me to Vinnytsia, where I hoped to connect with my soldier friends. As I waited in line for the driver to arrive, a couple asked me what service I was using. I showed them the contact on my phone. They gasped. "That's the driver who took our credit card information over the phone and failed to pick us up!"

Fortunately, I was not the trusting type. When the driver requested my credit card over the phone, I firmly told him that I would pay him in cash once the trip was complete. Although I successfully avoided his scam, I stepped into his car that morning knowing that he was a thief.

Chapter Twenty-Two

In ordinary circumstances, the drive from Zaporizhzhia to Vinnytsia takes fourteen hours. I paid the driver eighteen hundred hryvnia (US $61). It was yet another unpleasant drive, but for different reasons. The man was angry and unhinged. He drove at a speed of two hundred kilometers per hour in an impenetrable downpour of rain as music blared on the radio. He chain-smoked and cursed at Yola for the entire trip, complaining that her fur was shedding over the upholstered seat. I feared that he would slam on the brakes and throw us onto the roadside.

I ignored him and texted my soldier friends in Vinnytsia. Each time they saw my geolocation, they asked, "What, are you flying here on a plane?"

We entered the outskirts of Vinnytsia. The driver slammed on the brakes and dropped me off at a checkpoint.

"Get out," he barked. "Vinnytsia is right beyond that checkpoint. I'm not driving you any further after curfew. I don't need problems."

It was close to midnight. I looked around me, wondering where I would go next. Oddly, I felt no fear as I walked down the empty road. It may as well have been a warm sunny day on which I strolled down a country lane. I texted my soldier friends:

I HAVE 'GENERALLY' ARRIVED.

THE DRIVER REFUSED TO BRING ME INTO THE CITY. HE DROPPED ME OFF AT A CHECKPOINT IN SOME FIELD. TAKE ME OUT OF HERE AS SOON AS POSSIBLE. OTHERWISE, I'LL WALK TO VINNYTSIA ON FOOT.

They wrote back:

AHAHA, ADORIANA, STAY WHERE YOU ARE. YOUR GEOLOCATION CAME. DON'T EVEN THINK OF GOING ANYWHERE.

Ukrainian soldiers emerged from a small house at the checkpoint and approached me in the field. Their military working dog barked aggressively at Yola as they shined flashlights in my face. "Girl, how did you end up here?" they asked, staring at me and Yola in bewilderment.

Their native Ukrainian speech was music to my ears. The Ukrainian language is also called the nightingale language because it is smooth and melodic. In Mariupol, everyone spoke Russian.

"I'm from Mariupol," I answered. "Now my friends will come for me."

They were stunned and somewhat amused. They shook their heads and examined my papers. "Good night, girl! Do your friends know there is a curfew? Civilians aren't allowed on the streets and that includes you too. Come and stay at our post for the night. We'll take you into the city tomorrow."

"Can I stay here for a while?" I asked. "They'll come for me now."

The soldiers laughed. They probably wondered what kind of idiots would come for a deranged woman in a filthy red coat standing in a field with her dog after curfew. Suddenly, two armored vehicles with Ukrainian flags on top came barreling down the road. The vehicles stopped at the checkpoint and my soldier friends jumped to the ground and embraced me. I was over the moon! They all looked so beautiful in their fashionable uniforms, the design and colors of which indicated a much higher rank than the uniforms of the soldiers guarding the checkpoint.

"We'll take her to the city," they told the soldiers. No further questions were asked.

Now I am home, I told myself as I climbed into the armored vehicle. *My buddies from Mariupol are here.* I couldn't recover from happiness!

We went to the apartment where my friends were staying. The first order of business was to take a shower. I had not properly washed since visiting a stranger's apartment in Berdyansk. I absolutely stank. My friends gave me a huge men's shirt to wear. They quickly made sandwiches and poured me half a glass of vodka. "Drink it," they instructed gently.

We talked into the early morning hours. I told them about everything I witnessed in Mariupol. It was a prolonged and intensely emotional conversation. We laughed and cried, sometimes slipping into long stretches of silence as we remembered the past.

In Vinnytsia, I realized just how shattered my psyche had become. Being amongst friends did not reduce my insomnia or calm my mind. I continued to experience sharp mood swings that both surprised and frightened me. I was tearful all the time. A dark and very oppressive depression followed me as I walked the city streets with tears coating my face. I saw that life went on and it caused me to cry. I remembered what happened in the underground shelter and it caused me to cry. I passed a Ukrainian soldier on the sidewalk and my worry about him caused me to cry. Whenever I looked up at the sun, I wondered if a bomb would fall at any second, and guess what? That caused me to cry.

My soldier friends would come home for a few hours, either early in the morning or late at night. Needless to say, they were very busy men engaged in the fights of their lives. The front door to the house was made of heavy iron and it rattled whenever it opened or closed. My friends saw how I jumped and twitched every time the door made a noise, so they started to announce themselves whenever they entered the house. "I'm here. It's me."

While in Vinnytsia, I met with many Ukrainians who were eager to hear my firsthand account of what had happened in Mariupol. Everyone was talking about the beautiful port city that had become Russia's slaughterhouse. The losses were so large in number, it was almost impossible for Ukrainians to fathom. What could I tell them, other than to share my hope that all the Russians who took up arms and raped my native land would die slow and painful deaths?

Is the desire for such retribution poison to the human soul? All I know is I felt that vengeance with every inch of my being.

I also learned about what was happening at the Azovstal Steel Plant. In April, the steel factory was a refuge of last resort for beleaguered civilians hiding inside the vast maze of underground bunkers and tunnels. It was also the Ukrainian military's last foothold in our key port city.

Hundreds of civilians—mostly women, children, and the elderly—were trapped inside the plant alongside Ukrainian soldiers. They had very little food, no clean water, and no essential medicines. One soldier reported that what he wanted more than anything was a cup of fresh water. I knew the feeling. As with the leaders in the shelter where I stayed, the men tried to keep the spirits of the children up. It was a near-impossible task given what the youngsters, many of them newly orphaned, had been through. Weeks later, Mariupol's mayor would state, "If Mariupol is hell, Azovstal is worse."[34]

---

34. Hopkins, Valerie, Tiefenhaler, Ainara. "From Battered Mariupol Steel Plant, Fighters Share Desperate Videos to Push Out Story." *New York Times.* 29 April 2022. https://www.nytimes.com/2022/04/29/world/europe/mariupol-steel-plant-video.html

On my first day in Vinnytsia, I went to the supermarket for groceries. I could not concentrate on what I needed to purchase. An incomprehensible panic seized me. I eyed other shoppers walking by—making purchases, greeting neighbors, laughing, and chatting in small groups. Tears needled my eyes. How could anyone around me understand what it was like to be a stranger in a strange land—to have your entire identity torn asunder with no hope of ever returning home again?

Compounding my panic was the realization that the grocery store and its customers and workers could die at any moment. They may have felt safe, but the residents of Mariupol also felt relatively safe in the weeks before our city was leveled to the ground. I now understood the fragility of manmade structures and the illusory nature of life. In my mind's eye, I saw the supermarket in which I stood burning to the ground and the people inside scattered across the tiled floor like minced meat. *What is the point of all of this?* I wondered.

The fluorescent lights and noises made me dizzy. My chest tightened, lungs choking for breath. I felt like a dead woman who had been thrust back into the land of the living. I rushed out of the store and sat down on a bench. *Deep breath in… deep breath out…* I had never experienced panic attacks until the war began. By the time I left Mariupol, they were like an endless stream of unwanted guests pounding on my door.

I phoned my soldier friends. "Are you in the city?" I asked. "I don't feel well. I'm hyperventilating. Can you stop by the supermarket?"

They told me that they could not come to get me; I should call an ambulance. I'm not a fan of doctors, so I ended the call and mentally groped my way through the attack. As a way of slowing my racing thoughts, I bowed my head and focused on the slab of pavement beneath my feet, carefully tracing the cracks and bumps with my gaze. After several minutes of deep breathing and mental focus, I was able to step back inside the store.

That night, my friends gave me a pill to calm down and I downloaded a meditation app named Metitopia. I listened to the narrator and focused on his voice and then on myself. It worked. I felt so much better. The point of all of *this*, I realized, is to live in the moment. In the end, the present moment is all that any of us have. Don't fixate on the past. Don't worry about the future. Stay present.

Sadly, by the summer of 2022, the civilians of Vinnytsia were thrust into the nightmare of Putin's war. At least twenty people, two of them children, died in an attack by Russian Kalibr missiles launched from submarines in the Black Sea.[35]

35. Yeung, Jessie, Guy, Jack, Khalil, Hafsa, Upright, Ed. "It's mid-afternoon in Kyiv. Here's what you need to know." Live updates, Russia's War in Ukraine. *CNN.* 14 July 2022. https://www.cnn.com/europe/live-news/russia-ukraine-war-news-07-14-22/index.html

Chapter Twenty-Three

I intended to stay in Vinnytsia indefinitely but after talking to my soldier friends, I was reminded of the instability of the situation throughout Ukraine. My friends shot straight from the hip. "If you don't take up arms, Adoriana, then you interfere with our work."

They explained to me that in the villages near battlefields, residents endangered not only their own lives but also the lives of the soldiers. The soldiers had to change their plans and rebuild them over and over again so no civilians were harmed. Of course, I knew they were right.

In a perfect world, one in which money was no issue, I could have easily traveled to a city in western Ukraine. In the real world, however, such destinations were far beyond my nonexistent income and assets. Ukrainian landlords in western Ukraine were cashing in on the war, renting tiny apartments to families fleeing places like Kiev or Kharkiv for exorbitant sums of money. They knew renters were desperate. Some wanted to stay in Ukraine because they had a husband or a father or a son who was fighting and they needed to be close by, if only to see the soldier for a few hours per week. Others owned businesses in Ukraine. If they left, the business would disappear. Regardless, there was no way I could have afforded a thousand-dollar studio apartment.

There is a long-standing expression in Ukraine: "Someone is at war, and also someone's mother." It was said before the war to describe the people who profit from someone else's grief. No matter how warmly I may speak of Ukrainians, certain people care only about themselves. In Berdyansk, the bus drivers requested triple rates to take us to the ring by the field. You can be indignant, you can curse them till kingdom come, but the fact remained: they wanted to swindle your very last dime and you were powerless to do anything about it.

I recently read a thread on social media in which people discussed whether it was right for Ukrainian civilians to refuse to leave the regions in the greatest peril.

I wrote, "It is their choice. If there is an opportunity for them to leave and they choose not to leave, they will likely regret the decision and cry about it later. It is all very sad. Leaving your home and way of life is not as easy as it sounds. Many foreigners see refugees as freeloaders or even competitors."

Someone responded to my comment, "Okay, it's their choice, but what about the children? Why should they stay and die because their parents made a bad decision?"

She made an excellent point. Is it right to separate children from parents who refused to leave? There are no easy answers. However, there is something to be said about our duties as Ukrainians in a time of war. Civilians should feel compelled to do everything possible to get out of the way and let the military men and women do their job.

Not long after I participated in that online thread, the Ukrainian government mandated the evacuation of all civilians in Ukraine's Donetsk region. If a person refused to leave, they had to provide a written statement explaining the situation and wait for government approval to stay.

I searched online for refugee camps in Europe. It appeared Poland's humanitarian resources had been stretched thin, whereas the city of Ostrava in the Czech

Republic had many openings for incoming refugees. A few days later, I boarded a private bus in Vinnytsia and headed for the Czech Republic by way of Poland. Thankfully, the Ukrainian mobile provider, Kyivstar, offered very affordable roaming rates. I could easily utilize communications and access the internet outside of the country.

The line at the Polish border stretched for several kilometers. I did not mind. I was just grateful to finally have physical distance from the fighting. I heard crowds of people speaking Polish, a language with slightly different pronunciations than Ukrainian but similar in meaning.

A Polish security guard approached me and Yola. I grew nervous, thinking he would have a problem with me traveling with a dog. To my surprise, he pulled out his cell phone and showed me a photo of his husky. After encountering so many hostile Russian soldiers during my travels, it was both comforting and uplifting to receive such friendly warmth from a member of Polish law enforcement. My brief time spent in Poland showed me the Poles are truly fraternal people. They were the first to extend their hands to Ukrainians at the commencement of the war and, to my knowledge, they have shouldered the largest influx of refugees without complaint.

After crossing the Polish border, I arrived in the city of Katowice. The bus station did not resemble a refugee camp. People hurried about, focused on their own business. I walked to a nearby train station and located a young man wearing a distinctive vest indicating he worked as a translator.

"Excuse me," I asked in Ukrainian. "Where are the ticket offices?"

He had not worked at the rail station for long because he had no idea where the ticket offices were located. He called another Polish employee at the station and asked him in Polish to walk me to the box office. There, I was given a free train ticket to Ostrava.

I sat on the bench with Yola at my side and studied a large board on the wall that listed times of departures and arrivals. I grew anxious because my train was late. I located the young interpreter, and he asked a woman standing by the tracks if I was on the right platform. She reassured him that this was the correct platform for the train to the Czech Republic and not to worry, trains going to that country arrived every thirty minutes.

The train ride from Katowice, Poland, to Ostrava, Czech Republic, was remarkably easy. I had grown accustomed to endless checkpoints and delays in Ukraine. In comparison, the train from Katowice to Ostrava took a little over an hour without any stops. When I stepped off the train, no customs agents were asking to see my passport. I realized that, for travel purposes, Europe contained no borders—at least not for a Ukrainian refugee traveling in April 2022.

In Ostrava, I walked to a refugee reception center, where volunteers gave me a mobile operator card, toothbrush, shorts, socks, toothpaste, and anti-bacterial hand wipes. I could choose any clothing I needed from a few piles of donated secondhand garments. Volunteer interpreters helped refugees to prepare all of the necessary documents for entry into the country, namely health insurance, a temporary visa, and a bank account. The center also provided food coupons, which I could use to pay for tea, coffee, sandwiches, and cookies in the common room. While it was not homemade food, I was grateful. There were booths with MEDIC inscriptions at the camp where first-aid workers treated patients for conditions like high blood pressure and headaches and booths in which social workers provided counseling.

While I was impressed by the number of services freely provided to refugees, I knew such support would not last forever. The protracted conflict and Russia's "systemic attacks on health infrastructure" would likely result in many nurses and doctors leaving Ukraine and neighboring countries as they did in the Syrian conflict, causing further strain on the system.[36] Making matters worse, Ukraine was experiencing a polio outbreak before the war, and Russia's invasion disrupted the vaccinations of children throughout the country. The war also made it extremely difficult for cancer and HIV patients to find treatment, and the continuing spread of tuberculosis was another lethal threat to these medically compromised individuals.[37]

I stepped inside a MEDIC booth and told a nurse about my chronic cough. She gave me a potent cough syrup and vitamins. She told me they had run out of acetaminophen, but a new shipment would arrive the following day. That night, I joined other refugees, both sick and healthy, elderly and young, laying on cots in a huge hall that smelt of bleach and Lysol. The cough syrup worked wonders. For the first time in months, I was able to sleep half the night without coughing. I awoke at 2 a.m., took another swig, and slept like a baby until the sun came up.

While most of my fellow refugees were out the door the next morning, I stayed for two more days because of quarantine requirements for dogs. Yola was placed in a kennel with other incoming dogs. I was worried about how she would do without me, but she didn't seem to mind a bit. The animals were kept in separate enclosures. Workers watched over them all night, fed them twice daily, and even took them for long walks along the embankment. I felt a real kinship with those workers.

I was finally informed that it was my time for "distribution." I had no idea where they would take me and Yola. We boarded a bus and left the city. After a while, mountains appeared on the horizon. I love the mountains and knew something good awaited us.

36. "5 Health Crises" International Rescue Committee. 7 Apr 2022. https://www.rescue.org/article/5-health-crises-endanger-ukrainian-lives-war-continues
37. Ibid

Chapter Twenty-Four

The bus driver dropped us off at a remote ski resort in the quaint, mountainous village of Malá Morava. It appeared to offer just what I needed—nature, fresh air, peace, and rest. A woman approached the crowd and started calling off names from a list and distributing us into rooms at a nearby boarding house.

If you told me right before the invasion that I would be living in a ski resort in the Czech Republic within a matter of months, I would have called you crazy—but there I was, a transient living in an idyllic village that was home to only six hundred inhabitants before the war. My world had been turned upside down. As humans, we identify ourselves by where we live, what our homes and jobs are like, and the friends and family members who coexist with us. Without those external marking points, I felt as though my identity had been violently stripped away, despite the beauty of my surroundings. To the strangers I passed in the streets of Malá Morava, I was a nameless refugee who spoke a foreign tongue.

On the upside, many of the native residents of Malá Morava were quite welcoming. Early on, I walked with Yola past a house with a blue-and-yellow Ukrainian flag in the yard. A man came out to the porch. I shouted, "*Slava Ukraini!*" ("Glory to Ukraine!")

He answered, "Glory to the heroes!"

I assumed he was Ukrainian, but the man—who introduced himself as Lucas—informed me that he was Czech and had friends in Ukraine. Lucas had kind eyes and a welcoming smile. He had no idea how much his support of Ukraine meant to me.

On my first day in Malá Morava, I climbed a small mountain with Yola. In mid-April, the snow had mostly melted on the ground. The winter season was over, and the vacationing skiers had all cleared out. Light snow fell from a cloudy sky. Birds swiftly darted through the trees—woodpeckers, sparrow hawks, hawfinch, and many more. Ahead of us, a family of red deer crossed the path. They moved with such tranquility and grace as if one with nature—one with the universe. Yola was no different. She was glad to be in her element. She ran like a horse, chasing after squirrels and gnawing at the snow.

At that moment, I realized that I was walking with Yola through the very forest I had dreamt about on my last day in the shelter. It was not merely a fever-induced hallucination that had prompted me to leave the underground basement. It was a mystical vision.

In the weeks and months that followed, I experienced additional unexplained phenomena. For example, whenever I looked at a clock, I would see the numbers 11.11, 8.08, 15.15, and so on. In numerology, they're called angel numbers. Had I lost my grip on reality or was something else going on? Perhaps I was experiencing what psychologists call dissociation, whereby the mind of a traumatized person separates from reality. Sometimes I would wake in my bed in Malá Morava and think I was still in my bed in Mariupol. Waking up to the sound of explosions in the early morning hours of February 24 was a bad dream, and all of the chaotic events that followed were part of the nightmare. I would lie in bed and think, *I still have bathroom renovations to complete, and a few days of vacation left to enjoy.*

Then I would wipe the sand from my eyes and realize…
it wasn't a dream. It was real.

Yola and I reached the mountain's summit. The icy wind
was fierce at that high elevation. Though it stung my face
and gloveless fingers, my feet remained firmly planted on the
ground. I gazed in rapture at the valley below. *My God, am
I really alive?* I wondered. *Am I really here, surrounded by
so much beauty, so much peace? How can this be happening
to me? God, thank You for giving me the chance to survive.
I love this world so much!*

The fresh air smelt woodsy and refreshing. My heart
swelled with gratitude and pure joy. I simultaneously laughed
and cried. I fell to my knees and rolled about in the snow
with Yola, engrossed in the simplicity of the moment—a
simplicity that I would never have fully appreciated before
the war. I wanted to dissolve into everything around me in
that state of amazing lightness. I felt more alive than I have
ever felt in my life, as though all worldly problems did not
exist.

That euphoria came crashing down when a plane pierced
the sky directly above us. Yola instinctively pulled at the
leash. The sound of the plane flying in such close proximity
terrified both of us. Yola looked for a place to hide. In turn,
I wanted to sink into the ground and cover my ears with
my hands as I did whenever the loudest shelling occurred in
Mariupol. The plane went past us and disappeared back into
the clouds.

I stared down at the hodgepodge of log cabins and
Swiss-inspired chalets dotting the landscape below. My
eyes traced the path of the Moravice River flowing past
beech forests and clusters of spruce and pines. *I have lost
my home, my city, my life. What's to come of me now?* I
brooded anxiously.

We descended the mountain and entered the shelter.
The pattern of mood swings involving intense highs and
disconsolate lows was rapidly becoming my new normal.

In the span of five minutes, I could jump from jubilation to despair and then slip into a state of profound emotional numbness.

The numbness could last for hours, sometimes days. I would feel nothing, think nothing. The events of the last two months rendered me strangely catatonic. For example, I could be calmly eating a slice of toast, and the color of the jam would suddenly bring to mind the raw pulp of the man's shattered leg in the shelter. I would drop the toast onto the plate and vacantly stare into space. The numbness would last for hours—until an almost uncontrollable rage would emerge. I wanted to wail hysterically like a madwoman. *Why? Why? Why? Why?!* No matter how good my circumstances were, I always felt like it could all be taken away from me in an instant, just as I experienced in Mariupol.

My sensitivity to high-pitched sounds and explosions was a nuisance. I always loved a raucous summer storm, but now thunder and lightning affected me as they never had before the war. Fireworks and other sharp sounds, like a train's long, high-pitched whistle, sent me into a panic. I just hated it all. Every time a loud noise sounded, my heart instantly stopped. Then came the logical explanation that the unexpected noise was not a bomb falling or an anti-tank mine exploding.

I took small comfort in knowing I was not the only person afflicted with irrational fear. The hostel was located close to a small airport. Everyone reacted similarly when a plane flew overhead. We were all psychologically damaged by the war—some more than others.

***

As a northern breed, Yola thrived in the cooler mountain climate of Malá Morava. I would sometimes pour several packs of ice into the bathroom tub. Yola would rest overtop the glacial mound, sighing with contentment.

The boarding house where I stayed was a paint-peeled Victorian structure with rusted plumbing and poor heating. I was thankful to have a private room, but the arrangement was temporary. We were informed we would soon be transferred to a neighboring hostel, where five or six people shared one room.

I visited the hostel before moving in. The ramshackle building looked like it had not undergone any repairs since it was built in the 1800s. Inside, chaos reigned. The overcrowded rooms housed sick old women, stressed-out mothers with infants wailing in their arms, small children screaming and running haphazardly about, and women with dogs. The building was much colder than the one in which I was initially housed. There was no washing machine, and a small refrigerator was used by the hostel's twenty-seven occupants. I had to fish for a Wi-Fi connection in the streets. A single shower stood in a cavernous basement, covered in spiderwebs, although otherwise clean. I dreaded the day when I would have to use that shower, half fearing a repeat of the bloody shower scene in the movie *Psycho*.

I was always sick. Just when I recovered from one cold or flu, a new group of refugees would arrive and share their germs. The young children always had runny noses and high fevers. They placed their snotty hands over everything. They cried themselves to sleep and coughed through the night. I was placed in a small room contained within a larger room where the mothers and infants stayed. I constantly washed the floor of my tiny room and opened the window to let in fresh air to clear out the germs. My efforts were in vain as the mothers staying in the larger room did not clean the floors or open the windows. I had no choice but to walk through the infected space whenever I took Yola for a walk or needed to use the bathroom.

The mothers in the larger room utilized folk methods to treat their sick children so the stench of garlic filled the air. I encouraged them to take advantage of the health insurance we were given as refugees and to take their children to the doctor. The mothers dragged out the decision, resulting in everyone in the building getting sick. I was so relieved when that group left the larger room and moved to another area of the building. I was told that three refugees were scheduled to arrive that day. Two days passed. I asked if the three new refugees were still coming.

"There has been an unexpected delay," I was told. "The couple has a young child who became very sick. They'll arrive soon."

Terrific, I thought sarcastically. *Just terrific.*

I then engaged in a pity party that would make Winnie the Pooh's gloomy donkey friend Eeyore look like a downright optimist. I jotted down a list of pros and cons regarding my present-day circumstances.

The con column snaked down the page.

- I no longer lived in a beautiful and civilized city; I now lived in a remote forest.
- I was unemployed and was, for all intents and purposes, unemployable.
- Instead of a thousand-dollar monthly salary, I was given a modest allowance.
- Instead of a three-bedroom apartment, I lived in a crowded hostel.
- Instead of friends, I had dead friends or enemies.
- Instead of visiting my parents whenever I wished, I received one short message from them per month, and I constantly feared for their safety.

In contrast, the pro column had three words that overcame all my grievances.

- *I am alive.*

Chapter Twenty-Five

While many of the villagers welcomed us, others resented the sudden influx of refugees. To date, the Czech Republic has granted temporary protection status to more than three hundred thousand Ukrainian citizens since the start of the invasion. The number could reach half a million, about five percent of the country's total population, in the months to come. Our unexpected arrival has put a tremendous strain on the Czech social system, and the existing integration centers no longer have spare capacity.[38]

The Merriam-Webster Dictionary defines *"victim"* as follows:

1: one that is acted on and usually adversely affected by a force or agent
(a): one that is injured, destroyed, or sacrificed under any of various conditions
(b): one that is subjected to oppression, hardship, or mistreatment

According to the United Nations, over twelve million Ukrainians have fled their homes since the start of Russia's invasion. More than five million have fled to neighboring

---

38. "Czech Republic and CEB sign a grant of almost €400,000 to facilitate early integration of refugees from Ukraine" *Relief Web.* 21 April 2022. https://reliefweb.int/report/czechia/czech-republic-and-ceb-sign-grant-almost-400000-facilitate-early-integration-refugees

countries. Seven million people are displaced inside Ukraine.[39] Ukrainian refugees presently fleeing to other countries are victims of Putin's murderous invasion. At the expense of pointing out the obvious, very few people, myself included, are comfortable playing the role of victim. British comedian Ben Elton writes, "Sympathy for victims is always counter-balanced by an equal and opposite feeling of resentment towards them."[40]

I occasionally encountered such resentment while living in the Czech Republic. It came in many forms. As refugees, we were given free local bus passes. I stepped on a bus one day and presented my free pass to the driver. The man came close to blowing up with anger. He shot me an icy sneer and demanded to examine every page of the document. Dogs do not get to ride for free on buses, but most drivers waved Yola along without requesting I pay her fare. On that day, the livid man demanded I pay.

Similar incidents occurred when locals threw judgmental looks at new arrivals from Ukraine who wore nice clothing and drove decent cars.

"Sell the car!" some Czechs demanded. "Live on that money and not at the expense of our tax dollars. Stop walking with outstretched hands. Return to your country. Because of inflation, prices have risen for everything, and you make it worse. What kind of patriots are you if you leave your country in difficult times? There is no shelling in western Ukraine so stay there."

What they failed to understand was that the entire country was rife with instability. Just because bombs didn't fall in western Ukraine today did not mean they wouldn't

39. "How many Ukrainian refugees are there and where did they go?" *BBC News. Russian-Ukraine War.* 4 July 2022. https://www.bbc.com/news/world-60555472

40. Weinhold, Barry K. PhD, Weinhold, Janae B. PhD, *How to Break Free of the Drama Triangle and Victim Consciousness.* Colorado Springs, CO. CIRCL Press. 2017. p. 3. referencing.

fall tomorrow. For those casual observers, the war was like a TV program and Ukrainians like me were participants in the show. They could not grasp that some people lost everything, even identification documents.

Every refugee at the shelter where I stayed was given five thousand kronor (US $218.20) per month to purchase food and necessities. It was not easy for me to accept that money, knowing the umbrage that came along with it. Moreover, the complaints of many Czechs were not without merit. Some Ukrainians—who were not greatly affected by the war—went to European countries in their cars and received the same allowance as I did, renting expensive apartments in western Ukraine, and traveling back and forth between countries.

In addition to being resented as freeloaders, Ukrainian women were often targets of judgment and attacks from local women. I heard what they said. I saw how they glared. I couldn't help but give sidelong glances to such women and mutter sarcastically, "Oh, right, I'm here to pick up all of your men and take all of your jobs. I am such a threat…."

Now, more than ever, Ukrainian refugees represent the face of our nation to the people living in host countries. If one greedy Ukrainian takes ten toothbrushes from volunteers rather than one, or arrives in haute couture while receiving benefits, their greed is projected onto all of us. The critical words of others have the power to break a refugee's spirit. "You want a free toothbrush? What, so you can horde your stash and sell them?"

One woman abruptly left the hostel to return to her home in Kherson. "There are too many misunderstandings," she told me as she packed her bags. "I'd rather go home and die in my own house without being reproached for everything I do. I can't endure the humiliation."

So be it. She had made her choice. I had also made my choice. I would fight to live no matter what anyone said to me because I know who I am. We are all people on this

Earth and we live only once. Who knows what destiny has in store for any of us?

I once asked a Ukrainian warrior, "What if you hadn't gone to war?"

He answered, "I always think *what if*, Adoriana, but life is a series of choices. Will I regret my choices later? I don't know, but for now, I've made a choice."

***

Some Czechs referred to us as "gypsies," a racial slur for an ethnic minority of Romani people comprising about two to three percent of the Czech Republic's population. Originally migrants from northwestern India, the Romani (commonly known as the Roma) came to the region between the sixth and eleventh centuries. The Roma have endured significant hardship over the course of history. They were a target of Nazi extermination programs in World War II, and they were subjected to forced relocation during the Communist era.[41]

Today, the Roma are perceived by many in the white majority as having ten or more children, behaving immorally, stealing, demanding benefits without wanting to work, and defrauding the social system. Extremist right groups in the Czech Republic, like the Workers' Party of Social Justice, which garners about two percent of votes, have exploited the situation to raise support.[42] According to Miroslav Mareš, an expert on rightwing extremism at Masaryk University in Brno, the main strategy to raise support for the extreme right is to highlight criminal cases comprising members of the Roma population: Anti-gypsyism, where several local citizens who are not among the party's main support take part in various protest events

41. "Romani People" Wikipedia. 5 July 2022.
42. Mareš, Miroslav. "Right-wing extremism in the Czech Republic" *Friedrich Ebert Stiftung, International Policy Analysis* September 2012. p. 1 https://library.fes.de/pdf-files/id-moe/09347.pdf

focused on Roma criminality, is becoming the main area of contact of DSSS with mainstream forces.[43]

As of 2019, there was a seventy-percent unemployment rate amongst Roma in the Czech Republic. Roma who work for a living mostly fill unskilled and low-paying jobs.[44]

Some Hungarian Roma lived in Ukraine and had dual passports before the war. Many Ukrainians resented them for gaming the system, whereby they collected monetary benefits from Ukraine and the Czech Republic at the same time. When talk of Russia's impending invasion began, those carrying dual passports returned to the Czech Republic and settled in large cities like Prague and Ostrava.[45] This resulted in citizens native to Ukraine being sent to remote villages when they fled to the Czech Republic. The Czech cities simply did not have any more resources to offer.

I shared a room in the hostel with a young woman who phoned local agencies to request an apartment. She was refused when she told the representative that she was from Ukraine. "We had an unpleasant experience with gypsies carrying a Ukrainian passport," the man on the phone said.

"Adoriana, they think of us as gypsies," she lamented.

Addressing the myriad of contributing factors to the Roma's predicament in Western Europe and the menacing response of right extremist groups would require a doctoral thesis, and I am not here to do that. I am a tattoo artist and former merchandiser, not an academic. Rather, I bring this issue up to emphasize how pinched Czech relief programs were before the Russian invasion of Ukraine, and how the sudden and unexpected presence of hundreds of thousands of Ukrainian refugees presented daunting financial challenges

43. Ibid

44. "The Roma in the Czech Republic." Prague Guide. 16 May 2021. https://www.prague.fm/23139/the-roma-in-czech-republic/

45. "The Czech Republic introduces enhanced control of the provision of financial assistance to Ukrainian refugees" *Visit Ukraine Today.* 11 May 2022. https://visitukraine.today/blog/394/the-czech-republic-introduces-enhanced-control-over-the-provision-of-financial-assistance-to-ukrainian-refugees

to the country as a whole. I also tell you that being called a "gypsy" was another cruel reminder of the loss of identity, dignity, and respect that I had once taken for granted as a Ukrainian.

Chapter Twenty-Six

There were several highly educated refugees living in our shelter in the Czech Republic. A vibrant young lawyer named Kris arrived from Kiev with her sister and mother. They had fled after the initial bombing of the city at the beginning of the invasion. Now, Kris wished to return. The law firm where she had worked was still in business. Her family had a nice house, a nice income, and normal lives before the war. Adjusting to life as a refugee was simply too painful for them. Even the threat of death did not stop the family from eventually deciding to go back to Ukraine. Though Kris and I had become friends at the shelter, she left without saying goodbye.

Kris and her family were part of a growing trend whereby many refugees were choosing to return to Ukraine. On the surface, it seemed like insanity. Why go to the bother of fleeing a war-torn country only to return and risk dying? Nevertheless, if one still had a house or an apartment in Ukraine, the option to return was tempting. Some refugees reasoned that they would rather have a space where no one would kick them out into the streets, and a place where they still had family and friends than exist indefinitely in crowded foreign shelters.

This was especially true for the elderly. It takes a certain amount of youthful gumption to start life over from scratch. When people are old and lonely, they long for familiarity.

They are too tired to start over, especially in the face of so many obstacles, including language barriers. For many, the desire to return home was stronger than the desire to stay alive. That was certainly true of an infirm elderly grandmother who lived in the shelter. When her family members went out for a walk, she remained in the hostel brooding about wanting to return to her home in Poltava. She made her family so miserable with her cursing and complaining, they finally agreed to return with her to Poltava.

I corresponded with her granddaughter on Viber after they arrived in Poltava. "Granny has lost her mind," the woman said. "I'll be coming back to the Czech Republic soon. It's not safe here with my daughter."

"Will you leave your grandmother behind?" I asked.

"She has given us no choice, Adoriana. She is rooted to the ground. She says she has nothing else to live for, and she is prepared to die in her house."

In contrast, some refugees thrived on the opportunity to start life over in the Czech Republic.

A woman and her daughter recently left our camp in Malá Morava and moved into an apartment in the town of Gavirzhov, where she found a job working as a hairdresser. She dyed her hair a different color, got a tattoo with Czech insignia, and blossomed in her new environment. She did not have many clients at first, but soon, Ukrainians in the surrounding towns found out about her. She now has a list of regular clients, both Czech and Ukrainian. She told me that she began each morning with a spirit of gratitude.

"You need to build the ideal plan for your situation and clearly imagine how everything will be implemented in stages," she instructed. "It's all about mind over matter, Adoriana. I divorced my husband last year. You know, as terrible as this war has been, for me, it has also been a kind of salvation. I could not have rebuilt my life and forgotten him so easily if we were still in Ukraine. Being in the Czech

Republic has helped me to decide for myself. For the first time in a long time, I am free."

My feelings existed between those two extremes. I will never live in Mariupol again, even if Ukraine wins the war. The bad events that took place will always eclipse positive memories. I am also a realist. I understand that all of Ukraine will be littered with unexploded shells and landmines for years to come, the infrastructure will take decades to restore, and many Ukrainians will struggle with mental illness for the remainder of their lives. If everything that happened in Mariupol happened gradually, it would not have shocked people so much, but in a matter of days, hours—*even seconds*—our city and way of life were blasted to bits.

Still, I would love to visit Ukraine in peacetime. It will always be the place that feels most comfortable to me, and the country occupies a cherished chamber of my heart—but I refuse to fall into the trap of excessive nostalgia. Even while living in Mariupol, I frequently traveled to neighboring cities and countries, seeking out new places to discover and things to do. Back then, I did not have to worry about tomorrow. Ukrainian tourists were warmly welcomed because we were ready to spend our money. We were not viewed as second-class creatures. I'm glad I have been able to see the other side of the coin. Without money to rent hotel rooms and make purchases, we are treated very differently.

At last, I would celebrate my thirty-second birthday in a matter of weeks. Decades of life stretched out before me. I was determined to lay the dark memories to rest and carve out a productive and meaningful existence. Putin may have destroyed my magnificent native city but he would not destroy my spirit.

***

I kept in regular touch with my older sister, Inna, who had moved to the United States long before the war. Inna was not in a position to sponsor me as a refugee and fly me to America. She was a single mother and struggled to make ends meet. She and I also got into fights about the war over the phone.

"Ukraine won't win," Inna said. "Russia has more weapons and soldiers. Russia is much stronger than Ukraine."

I was shocked. I screamed and cried. "Don't say that! Russia must never win!"

Inna thought I had lost my mind. "What has happened to you, Adoriana?" she asked.

She did not want to hear about my problems. She had too many of her own. However, she knew an American woman, Laura, who wanted to help me. Laura frequently asked Inna how I was doing. Laura reassured me that she did not agree with Inna; she strongly supported Ukraine. Much to my surprise, Laura emailed and sent me money via Western Union.

The boots that I wore upon arrival in the Czech Republic were made of high-quality leather, and I had only purchased them in December 2021. They now resembled relics from World War II: saturated with blood, riddled with burn holes, faded from chemicals. I was happy to throw them into the garbage, along with the stinky coat I had worn underground. So many bad memories. So many foul reminders. With part of the money that Laura sent, I was able to purchase new shoes and some used clothing from a thrift shop. I also visited the beauty salon for a haircut and style. It baffled me that a woman, whom I had never met, wanted to give me money with no strings attached. I was incredibly grateful.

When I arrived in the Czech Republic in April, the few jobs that remained available to non-English speaking refugees were the ones made available to the Roma population. For example, I was offered work in a cold shop for twelve hours per day, six days per week, cutting meat. The job involved heavy lifting and standing. Eighty percent of the salary I was offered would cover a shabby apartment. The remaining twenty percent of my salary would cover food and other essentials. Accepting that job would entrap me into a cycle of poverty with no way out.

I went to the nearest employment center located a half hour from the village. They gave me a printout of job vacancies from an outdated database. I went to every address. Half of the vacancies were no longer valid; the jobs had long since been filled. The other half involved similar hours and demands as the job at the cold shop with even less pay. None would provide enough money to rent a decent studio apartment. I then visited a refugee center and requested housing in the city. I was told there was no longer social housing.

In the end, remaining in the Czech Republic was a dead-end proposition. The monthly minimum wage associated with a full-time job in that country was 16,200 kronor, the equivalent of US $689.47. I was offered a job in the kitchen of the refugee center for eight thousand kronor. However, the lowest monthly rent for an apartment was at least nine thousand kronor, so taking that job would result in having to stay in a crowded hostel indefinitely, and who knew when the Czech's goodwill would evaporate and we would be asked to leave?

I quickly concluded I needed to do two things to improve my dismal situation. First, I needed to leave the Czech Republic and move to a country with greater opportunities. Second, I needed to learn English straight away—and by straight away, I mean *stat*.

My mood in those days was nothing short of shitty. When I relocated from the boarding house to the overcrowded hostel, my sense of helplessness increased. Yes, I had to move to another country, but which one? And how would I find the money to travel, or a safe place to stay? Adding to my shitty mood, the people I lived with were constantly quarreling. The air was thick with stress and the stench of dirty diapers. I had purchased cream for my coffee and stuffed it into the back of the little fridge. Surprise, surprise! The cream was gone the next morning.

I asked everyone in the kitchen, "Who took my cream?"

They all stared back at me with *what? who, me?* looks on their faces.

That evening, someone told me who stole the cream. I confronted the woman. She claimed that she thought the cream was hers and that she would buy me a new carton of cream to replace what she drank.

"What the hell?" I muttered. I knew it was a petty problem, but there were so few things to look forward to that drinking my coffee with cream was one of them.

The following day, I went to remove my hand-washed clothing from the dryer. The clothes were nowhere to be seen. "Where are my clothes?" I shouted.

"Calm down, Adoriana," one woman said. "We have already taken them out of the dryer and put them in your room."

I returned to the room I shared with four others and found a mound of damp clothing smelling of mildew on my bed.

These troubles were admittedly trivial, not unlike what college students experience in a dormitory. However, given the events of the last two months, my nerves were wasted. Any little thing could trigger my simmering fury. To remedy the problem, I made a habit of leaving the hostel with Yola first thing every morning and returning late in the evening to avoid others.

In my free time—and I had a lot of free time—I walked to a local café with Wi-Fi and searched online for useful activities to pursue in the Czech Republic. I took advantage of the free travel pass offered to Ukrainian refugees and visited all of the cities in the Moravian region. I also visited several local charities. Caritas serves the victims of the War in Ukraine in many practical ways: housing, food, transportation, and medical care. I was especially interested in an operation organized by the local Czech volunteer who had the Ukrainian flag in his yard. Lucas had turned his home and garage into a makeshift warehouse, where military equipment was repaired for Ukrainian fighters.

Lucas's mother and wife sewed military uniforms for Ukrainian soldiers. This wonderful family also created items like bulletproof vests and silencers that, along with medicines, were shipped to Ukraine. They agreed to deliver boxes of items to my friends who were volunteering in Ukraine, and my friends agreed to hand the items over to the military. I can say with confidence that these precious commodities were not lost along the way or resold on the black market. I was bursting with happiness when I left Lucas's home. In one small way, I'd made a difference.

Meeting Lucas and his family was yet another experience that restored my faith in humankind. You may be surprised when I say that I have much greater optimism concerning humanity as a whole than I did a year ago. Before the war began, petty grievances caused me to pessimistically conclude that most people were selfish and troublesome. However, since the start of 2022, I have witnessed more noble acts of self-sacrifice and basic human kindness than I had witnessed in three decades on this Earth. I am now convinced that saints and angels walk among us. Yes, we all have character flaws, even the angels, and criminals also abound. I can personally attest to that fact. However, the key is to embrace faith and hope at all turns. One must never give up, even when it seems that everything is lost. Sunshine follows even the worst of storms.

Chapter Twenty-Seven

Masha was a sixty-five-year-old retired schoolteacher who lived with me at the shelter. Masha and her husband had fled the Donetsk Oblast region. They planned to return to the apartment they had lived in for decades in Svitlodarsk as soon as the fighting ended. Their son was fighting for Ukraine in the war, and they feared for his life. Masha approached me on a rainy morning at the end of May.

"Adoriana," she wept, "now we have nowhere to return, like you. Our city of Svitlodarsk has been captured. A neighbor phoned and told me that my apartment was broken into by the Russian soldiers. They are living in my home!"

Masha represented so many refugees who still held hope that their exile from Ukraine was temporary. As Russia relentlessly pounded the Donbas and occupied more villages and cities by the month, the hopes of refugees wanting to return to their homes in that region dwindled to the size of a mustard seed.

My conversation with Masha was deeply distressing. It stayed with me for days. I couldn't shake the fear that all of Ukraine would one day suffer the fate of Mariupol and Svitlodarsk. I thought of how Masha must feel, knowing Russian soldiers were in the private space she once called home—eating the little food that was left in her cupboards on her blue willow dinner plates, sleeping in her marriage bed, shitting into a toilet that would not flush.

There are many videos on social media where Ukrainians show what Russian soldiers have done to their homes. I don't believe this is fake information since so many people living in different areas have posted similar images. One video showed a huge plasma television the Russians were not able to take off the wall, so they shot bullets through the screen and defecated in the middle of the room and on the sofa. Other videos showed trashed children's rooms and broken furniture.

When I used to visit cities and villages in Russia before the war, I was alarmed to see so many filthy apartments and homes that resembled broken-down shacks. Cleanliness does not depend on wealth. A can of paint is relatively cheap, and a broom can be made from branches and straw. There is no excuse for such sloth. For this reason alone, the Russians' self-perception of being "better" than Ukrainians, in a class above us, is laughable. What Russian soldiers have done inside Ukraine since the war began is a manifestation of their essence—how they live in their own country.

Tell me, if a group of men invaded your property and claimed it for themselves, would you consider them to be thieves? What if they destroyed your valuable belongings? Would you want them prosecuted to the highest degree possible for the crime? Of course you would. The Russian soldiers are not just slovenly, they are thieves.

My thoughts turned to my apartment in Mariupol. Unlike Masha, I never entertained hopes of returning to my native city. Russian occupiers had already dismantled the buildings in the seventeenth to twenty-third micro-districts, and the building where I once lived was included in that list.[46] Now Russians were constructing five-storied structures in haste, using the cheapest materials. These buildings are intended

---

46. "Occupiers dismantle houses and garages in Mariupol." *0629.com.ua.* 21 July 2022. https://www.0629.com.ua/news/3430415/okupanti-demontuut-budinki-ta-garazi-v-mariupoli

to house the herd managers, but what about the homeless people of Mariupol?

I saw on the Mariupol city website that most people still cook their food over open fires and live off the rotten humanitarian stew that Russia gives them. Russia's hurried attempts at installing electrical wiring have resulted in countless fires. Most of the remaining residents are elderly, as well as those who have deluded themselves into believing that *the Russian world* will soon transform the city into a Leninist paradise.

Sadly, Mariupol is destined to become like Donetsk after Russia's 2014 annexation of Crimea, arrested in time and development. When I visited Donetsk as a child, the city teemed with young people and vibrancy. People went there to study, work, and attend festivals and concerts. What happened to Donetsk after Russia arrived?

Nothing.

Progress ceased altogether. Many residents migrated to free Ukrainian territories as Donetsk suddenly resembled the grim dystopian setting of *The Handmaid's Tale*. Like the Republic of Gilead in Atwood's novel, Donetsk was a ghost city under the rule of bandits with thieves' laws. I remember how people from Donetsk would visit Mariupol to buy toilet paper and laundry detergent because the cost of items cost was three times higher in Donetsk.

In the case of Mariupol, the decline in culture and infrastructure will be so much worse as there is nothing left of the city. I take solace in knowing that Russian soldiers will never live off the spoils of my parents' hard-earned money in the apartment we once called home.

An old friend from Mariupol recently wrote to me. "You don't talk to Russians?" he asked.

I was a little taken aback by such a question. "No," I wrote.

He answered me, "It's a pity that you survived."

I was shocked. My old friend had been bitten by Russian zombies and now brainlessly stumbled through the wreckage of Mariupol with stretched-out arms and a vacant stare in his eyes. Snarling and hissing. Groaning and grunting. His ignorance convinces him he is superior to most Ukrainians because he keeps in line with and vows allegiance to a ruthless madman.

***

People at the shelter often warned me to not watch the news. "It will trouble your nerves," they said. Still, I could not keep myself from going online and searching for updates about the war. After all, my parents were still in Ukraine, along with many friends who were fighting or assisting in humanitarian ways.

I was disheartened to see that Russia had resumed bombing Kiev in early June.[47] *Dear God, why won't they leave us alone?* I was horrified to see the Russian government was issuing Mariupol residents Russian passports.[48] The residents who remained in the ruined city were still without running water and electricity. They were forced to dismantle the mess the Russians had created. The Russians brought cars with large TV screens into the streets to present propaganda videos about how well the people of Mariupol will soon live in "Mother Russia."

I was relieved to learn that the women and children remaining beneath the steel plant in Azovstal had finally been evacuated in early May, although I was dismayed to later learn that over one thousand Ukrainian servicemen who had surrendered at the plant were transported to Russia

47. Myre, Greg. "Russia bombed a railcar repair facility in Kyiv." *NPR.* 5 June 2022. https://www.npr.org/2022/06/05/1103168586/russia-bombed-a-railcar-repair-facility-in-kyiv

48. "Invaders offering Russian passports to residents of Ukraine's Zaporizhzhya, Kherson Oblasts" *Yahoo! Finance.* 11 June 2022. https://finance.yahoo.com/news/invaders-issuing-russian-passports-residents-154200738.html

as prisoners of war and have now been subject to aggressive interrogations.[49] I fear for the safety of those heroic men.

Every day, I prayed for all of our Ukrainian soldiers. How beautiful and strong they are. They could give a wonderful future to this planet, yet they die every day. Every time I hear about more dead Ukrainians, both soldiers and civilians, it's as if the anger and pain are scalding me with boiling water. Only thanks to the fact that good conquers evil does our planet exist.

Even now, I see very little hope for the situation in Ukraine unless Putin dies of natural causes, and a changing of the guard takes place. As thousands of body bags carrying Russian soldiers pile up, the Russian population may come to realize the futility of Putin's war. I see that many people in Russia, including top deputies, do not support him. This gives me hope that they are *people,* not zombies. Perhaps a new regime would be willing to resolve the issue with Ukraine in our favor.

I'm not holding my breath, however. In early June 2022, Putin compared himself to Peter the Great, who waged the Great Northern War for twenty-one years. Putin claimed that, like Peter the Great, he was on a historical quest to "win back Russian lands."[50] He is in it for the long haul, regardless of the rapidly expanding loss of human life. Honestly, with so much blood on his hands, I don't know how the man sleeps at night. Has he no conscience, no soul?

Many have called Russia's invasion a war of attrition, whereby continuous losses in manpower, equipment, and supplies grind the enemy down to such an extent that soldiers

49. Pennington, Josh, Ritchie, Hannah. "More than 1,000 Ukrainian Soldiers from Mariupol transported to Russia, state media says." *CNN.* https://www.cnn.com/europe/live-news/russia-ukraine-war-news-06-08-22/ h_80b42ba5000bf1cb745896cb83c30f29

50. "Hailing Peter the Great, Putin draws parallel with mission to 'return' Russian lands." *Reuters.* 9 June 2022. https://www.reuters.com/world/ europe/hailing-peter-great-putin-draws-parallel-with-mission-return-russian-lands-2022-06-09/

lose their will to fight. There is no question that Putin is pursuing a war of attrition, but his ugly tactics go far beyond the battlefields. In committing endless criminal acts against Ukraine's civilian population, Putin has added a secret sauce to his war: terrorizing all Ukrainians. Women. Children. The elderly. Scaring the shit out of everyone. Letting them know that no place is safe. No city. No school. No hospital. No synagogue. No mosque. No church. No nuclear power plant nor the surrounding villages sharing the air.

Just when you least suspect it, a shell will drop from the open skies and rip apart the entire fabric of your existence. If this war had a soundtrack, it would resemble that of another classic slasher film: *ki ki ki... ma ma ma...ki ki ki ma ma ma...*

How Putin plans to fund his euphemistically titled *special military operation* in the years to come is anyone's guess. According to one source, "almost three times as many Russian millionaires are expected to leave the country (in 2022) than in 2019."[51] In that same article, Andrew Amoils, head of research at analytics company New World Wealth, asserted that Russia was "hemorrhaging millionaires."[52] Amoils ominously added, "If one looks at any major country collapse in history, it is normally preceded by a migration of wealthy people away from that country."[53]

An additional obstacle for Putin involves how he plans to rule over the hearts and minds of Ukrainians who have lost so much in the face of this barbarous invasion. It is one thing to invade a peaceful country, pummel its civilian structures, and carry out mass genocide; it is quite another to indefinitely rule over the remaining residents, most of whom despise you and all you stand for.

---

51. Cooban, Anna. "Russia is 'hemorrhaging' millionaires." *CNN Business.* 14 June 2022. https://www.cnn.com/2022/06/14/business/russia-millionaire-exodus/index.html

52. Ibid.

53. Ibid.

Putin has repeatedly stated that Russia is not threatening any country with nuclear weapons, but nuclear weapons will be employed if Russia's "sovereignty is threatened."[54] Since he has made it clear he does not care about the lives of Ukrainian civilians, what's to keep him from one day using tactical nuclear weapons, biological warfare, or chemical warfare in Ukraine, especially once he realizes that Russia is losing the war? The fallout would drift into Poland and the crisis could easily open the door to the commencement of World War III. The possibility of a nuclear attack on Sweden or Finland in retaliation for joining NATO could also ignite Putin's atomic wrath.

The Irish say, "Put your troubles in a bag and drop them over the bridge on your way over here." It is a cheerful adage that I found impossible to follow during my time in the Czech Republic. How could I put the troubles afflicting all Ukrainians in a bag and toss it away? I may as well have ripped out my heart and thrown it over a bridge.

My heart that aches for the people still living in Mariupol. There was an outbreak of cholera and dysentery in the early summer of 2022. Exposed corpses rotted beneath the hot sun. Only two to three percent of the city had running water, forcing people to wash clothing in street puddles and drink water from dirty wells. The conditions were medieval. I saw videos on TikTok documenting the *generous hand* of Russia to residents. Soldiers tossed food at crowds as though they were dogs, and set up four booths from which barrels of water dripped over people who needed to wash. God, I was shocked. Was this possible in my previously prosperous city? No, I simply could not accept it. How fortunate I was

---

54. "Russia will use nuclear weapons to defend sovereignty." *Business Standard*. 18 June 2022. https://www.business-standard.com/article/international/russia-will-use-nuclear-weapons-to-defend-sovereignty-says-putin-122061800213_1.html

to escape when I did. By June, the city was in quarantine, and no one was allowed to travel outside of it.[55]

Maybe the people in the hostel were onto something. I should have stopped looking at online news and social media. Doing so triggered panic attacks. I worried I would never see my parents again. I anxiously wondered how I would learn to fit into a foreign culture. Would I ever *belong* in a place again? Whenever the panic seized me, I firmly told myself, *snap out of it, Adoriana. Either you live, or you don't. It's your choice.*

The notion of having the freedom to choose where I would go and how I would live sustained me as I tried to untangle the web of trauma in my mind. Did Ukrainians who agreed to settle in Russia's filtration camps still have choices to make? No, their choices were now made for them by an autocratic regime.

That, in a nutshell, is what Ukraine is fighting for—*the right to choose* how one will spend their days on this Earth. It is a basic human right that only democracy can provide. Without freedom of choice, the human spirit dies.

55. Hunder, Max. "Cholera and other diseases could kill thousands in Ukraine's Mariupol- Mayor." *Reuters*. 10 June 2022. https://www.reuters.com/world/europe/cholera-other-diseases-could-kill-thousands-ukraines-mariupol-mayor-2022-06-10/

Chapter Twenty-Eight

Sometimes, what a woman needs is a day at the spa. While I could not afford to stay at a luxury spa and enjoy a massage or swim in a saltwater pool, I could at least travel to one and walk about the grounds with my best buddy, Yola.

In early June, I spent forty kronor (US $1.69) to travel to Karlova Studánka, a mineral spa in the Hrubý Jeseník Mountains. The state-owned facility employed treatments that were popular in the nineteenth century, with an emphasis on offering a clean-air environment to those suffering from non-tuberculosis respiratory diseases.[56]

Having come from the dusty city of Mariupol and endured five weeks in a chemically fraught basement with over two hundred sick occupants, I definitely would have benefited from the carbonic baths and mud wraps the spa offered its clientele. Alas, as an impoverished refugee, I would have to accept a simpler treatment.

A timbered drinking pavilion built in 1895 marked the location of the Wilhelm Spring, where a cascading waterfall reached twenty meters in height. Cliffs provided panoramic views of the verdant hills and timbered spa houses built in an Empire style. Thanks to the altitude of eight hundred meters above sea level, and the surrounding unspoiled forests, the air was the cleanest I have ever breathed.

---

56. *Visit Czech Republic, Karlova Studanka.* https://www.visitczechrepublic. com/en-US/9061b4e6-f092-411c-bec3-a0c6f41e231d/place/t-karlova-studanka

Yola and I sampled the free mineral water from one of the taps. The carbonated beverage carried a slight flavor of iron. I imagined the magical elixir sending healing energy to my weary limbs as I swallowed it down. What I would have given to drink such water during those horrid weeks trapped beneath the auto parts store!

I turned from the tap to see an elderly Czech couple smiling at me. The toned wife sported a tie-dyed shirt and matching cap. Like most women in the region, she wore no makeup. Her husband's blue eyes twinkled with affection. A long white ponytail reached the middle of his spine, giving him a hippie look. Both wore dungarees and hiking boots. The trendy couple illustrated the youthful exuberance of older people in the Czech Republic: physically active, skiing in the winter, swimming in the summer, and hiking year-round.

I worked at the hostel with a youthful seventy-five-year-old Czech woman who had the energy and health of a thirty-year-old. She told me about the heavy metal concerts she would attend throughout the Czech Republic, wildly dancing and body surfing above the crowd. I was shocked. My parents detested heavy metal music. My mother would shout, "Turn off those Satanists immediately!"

In Ukraine, the concept of old age meant that at sixty, you should look like you're one hundred and lead a lifestyle similar to preparing for a rainy day. Even if one had a good pension and worked hard in their youth, "rickety grandparent" status instantly fell upon them in retirement. I believe the poor ecology in Ukraine contributes to the mindset, along with societal influence.

There were many other cultural differences between the Czech Republic and Ukraine. I asked my Czech friend, Lucas, "Why don't you have playgrounds for your children? Why do ninety-nine percent of people drive cars made by

Skoda?[57] Why don't young women paint their lips with lipstick, or wear heels rather than boots or sneakers all the time?"

Lucas replied, "We are a modest people. We believe that there is no need to stand out, especially in a small town. If you happened to buy a Porsche, others will look askance at you."

The Czech mindset baffled me. In Ukraine, if a person could afford to drive a Porsche, no one looked askance at them. On the contrary, each person strove to be the best version of themselves, and every year, our country became better and better—until February 24, 2022.

"Good, yes?" the old hippie asked me of the water. That he spoke Russian did not surprise me. The older generation studied Russian as children in school.

"Yes, very tasty," I replied in Russian, the second tongue of many Ukrainians. I had become accustomed to miming movements like a silent-film actress whenever I needed to communicate with locals, so it was nice to finally communicate with a Czech in a shared language.

"It's a very rare occurrence when water tastes like carbonated," he said. "I never knew that we had a similar source of mineral water in our homeland until I went on a mountaineering expedition in the Caucasus and there was also such water—not from a tap. You had to climb down into the gorge to find it."

We spoke for a while, and I bid the couple farewell. The man said, "*Spasibo*," meaning "thanks" in Russian.

I responded, "No, in Ukraine we have the same word for *thanks* as you do in the Czech Republic. The word is *diakujiu*. It is spelled differently than your version, but it sounds similar."

His face lit up with the acquisition of new knowledge. "Yes, in Czech, it is also true. *Diakujiuo!*"

---

57. Skoda is a vehicle brand based and manufactured in the Czech Republic.

Yola and I hiked for a few hours until the slate gray sky split open with a heavy downpour of rain. I ran with her to the bus stop and sat down on a bench. A homeless man approached carrying loads of garbage bags that appeared to contain his personal belongings. He dropped his makeshift luggage to the gravel and started to crawl beneath the bench. I yelped with fright. I had not seen a single homeless person since arriving in the Czech Republic. In Mariupol, there were many homeless people, and I was quite used to seeing them in the streets, so it wasn't anything new to me. Rather, it was a new experience for me in the Czech Republic.

The haggard old man saw the fear on my face and apologized profusely and repeatedly. "I'm just reaching for this empty bottle to put it in the recycling bin," he said.

I suppressed a laugh. Not only were homeless people rare in this mountainous region of the Czech Republic, but evidently, they also cared about the environment.

The bus arrived. Yola followed me up the steps and immediately crawled under the seat, as she was accustomed to doing during all of our travels.

The bus driver turned and asked me, "Where did your dog go?"

"Don't worry," I said. "She's under the seat. She won't make a sound, not even a rustle." I spoke the truth. The only bad thing that Yola had ever done was chew apart one of my sneakers when she was a puppy. In her defense, she was teething.

The bus quickly filled with happy vacationers and left the village. Though most were Czech natives, they took endless photos of their landscape from the bus. I was growing quite fond of the Czechs. They drank inexpensive beer from the local breweries; the women wore Bohemian garnets mined in the region. Mostly blood-red in hue, the gemstones also come in black and green and there is a transparent type as well.

I gazed out the window at the forested hills painted in brilliant shades of green. I slid back on the upholstered seat, closed my eyes, and listened to the steady tapping of rain on the metal roof. A sudden surge of depression washed over me. My birthday was days away. I remembered how I'd celebrated with my friends in Mariupol the year before. It seemed like a movie to me now. Many of those friends were presently fighting for Ukraine. I didn't even know if some of them were still alive. A terrifying emptiness gnawed at me. I recalled Luda's words when I arrived at her apartment shortly following the first round of bombs: "Where to go? What to do?"

Three months later, I was haunted by the same two questions. *Where to go? What to do?*

Back at the hostel, I prepared a cup of mint tea with valerian extract to help me sleep. I undressed and slipped into the satin nightgown that Nina had given me. I wrapped my body in her soft white bathrobe, warmed by the memories of my two angels from Nikolske. I crawled into bed as Yola crept beneath the rusted metal frame where she felt safe. I put in earbuds and listened to my meditation app. The narrator's soothing voice did little to tranquilize my troubled mind.

Have you ever longed for a medical procedure that could erase all of the dark and traumatic memories from your mind? A procedure like the one used by the couple in *Eternal Sunshine of the Spotless Mind,* whereby the memories of a soured romance were deleted, or the program in the thriller series, *Severance,* in which one's memories are bifurcated into work memories and nonwork memories?

I wished I could have a memory-erasing chip installed in my brain—one that deleted all data downloaded since February 24, 2022. With such a chip, I could finally fall asleep and wake refreshed. I would even opt for the *Severance* device, allowing myself half of the day to recall the war and the other half to live in blissful ignorance. For now, I would have to rely upon my herbal friends, valerian drops and mother's wort.

***

While in the Czech Republic, I got in the habit of waking before dawn to walk Yola along a village road that led to the river. I absorbed the silence. Not a single car passed us. By mid-June, nature had erupted with life. The buds on the trees had bloomed. Colorful wildflowers sprinkled the forests and fields. I bent down to brush my fingers over the dewy blades of grass that lined the roadway and silently repeated a mantra from my meditation app: *Every day in every way, I am getting stronger.*

As part of getting stronger, I scheduled a dental visit in a nearby city for later that afternoon. I have always been disciplined about maintaining my oral health. In Mariupol, I used a toothpaste called Splat. Ironically, Splat is a Russian brand. Splat toothpaste has a perfect composition, free from sodium lauryl sulfate and saccharin. It doesn't contain synthetic antiseptic agents either. Splat was not available for purchase in the Czech Republic—even if it was, I would never again purchase a tube of Splat and give one cent to the Russian economy.

My oral health had rapidly declined from the weeks in the shelter beneath the auto parts store. I did not brush my teeth during that time. The chronic dehydration and stress also injured the health of my gums, not to mention the sugary diet of chocolate and stale waffles. By the second week of the invasion, I had developed stomatitis, a painful condition involving the swelling and inflammation of the gums. By the fourth week, tartar appeared.

My complexion was also a disaster. Soon after I arrived in the Czech Republic, a rash of pimples spilled over my face. Perhaps it was caused by stress or climate change. I also felt like I had aged ten years since the invasion. New wrinkles now appeared beneath my eyes and around my mouth.

As Yola and I returned from our early morning stroll, an excitable black dachshund named Alu greeted us outside the hostel. When Alu and her Ukrainian owner first arrived, Alu did not get along with Yola. She always tried to grab Yola's leg with her mouth. She tried to grab my leg too. However, after a few days, Alu and Yola became great playmates.

Yola leapt with enthusiasm and charged after her new friend. I watched as they frolicked in the grass and sped about in circles playing games of catch-me-if-you-can.

Above us, a rising sun cast bright red-and-lemon-yellow streaks over the heavily forested mountaintops.

It is worth fighting for such moments, I thought. *Happiness consists of simple pleasures.*

Chapter Twenty-Nine

I baked two biscuit cakes on my birthday and shared them with all of the refugees in the hostel. Each slice was a small peace offering on my behalf, as if to say, through sugar and flour, *let's put petty differences aside and try to get along.* Everyone was grateful and pleasantly surprised.

Nonetheless, no amount of cake prevented my eviction to the dreary attic above. Other refugees complained about Yola. Some of the women were allergic to dogs. They said that Yola's fur appeared on their clothing when they removed it from the dryer. A few others did not like dogs— no matter how clean, quiet, or calm. High-strung children screamed in terror when we silently walked past. Poor Yola couldn't catch a break.

And so, I complied with the request. What other options did I have—a luxury ocean cruise to the Mediterranean? An extended holiday in Bora Bora? I didn't mind going to the attic because there's nothing I wouldn't do to hang on to Yola. No matter how difficult it is to travel across borders with a dog, I am one hundred percent committed to her. That commitment was solidified when shells were flying and we were shot at in the street outside the basement shelter in Mariupol. Without question, Yola saved my life that night. She is a part of me—the only living creature to whom I can express my problems, the only living creature who consistently makes me smile.

I gathered our meager belongings and trudged upstairs. How different my thirty-second birthday was from past birthdays, which always began with a phone call from my parents. Every year, they told me the same pleasant story about how cherries ripened everywhere on the day I was born. When we ended the call, I indulged in a hot and foamy bath while sipping a glass of champagne. Depending on the year, I would either dress up to travel someplace different or go to a fancy restaurant with friends.

Regrettably, those days were gone.

The attic was full of spiderwebs. I was not in a position to complain, however. Though run-down, the hostel was clean. Lucas had brought us an extra refrigerator and washing machine the week before, and we had set up a system in which refugees were assigned jobs cleaning the common room, kitchen, and toilets daily.

The mattresses that were given to refugees were each packed in an oilcloth. We were not permitted to remove the oilcloth. Perhaps they planned to resell the mattresses when we were finished with them, or maybe they were vigilant about not having the mattresses stained. Regardless, I don't recommend sleeping on an oilcloth. The waterproof fabric rustles with any motion, and your back soaks with sweat.

Life in the crowded hostel stretched into July. New refugees sporadically appeared, furthering the stress and commotion. Early one evening, seven refugees arrived at our doorstep, including a woman with two toddlers. The young mother looked like a deer caught in the headlights as she stared in horror at the bedlam surrounding her. She stated that she and her children had not eaten all day. It took over a week for them to get out of Ukraine and she did not have a cent left to her name. She began to panic and sob.

I knelt at her side. "I know it's difficult," I consoled her, "but you need to stay calm for the children. I will give you some money for food until your government allowance arrives."

"My children need special food," she wept frantically. "I'm told the buses don't run after 4 p.m. How will I purchase food for tonight?"

"Didn't they ask about your needs at the refugee center before sending you here?" I asked.

She looked at me like I was crazy. "What refugee center? There was a building full of gypsies and we were put on a bus and taken here without knowing where we were headed. No one told us anything. We were offered no food, no money."

I realized how fortunate I was to escape Ukraine in April when the refugee centers in Poland and the Czech Republic still had ample resources to assist refugees. As the war ground on, such services and resources were depleted, leaving refugees like this young mother empty-handed. I located Lucas, and he drove her into town to purchase supplies that night.

"How do I get out of here?" she later cried to me, as if sentenced to Siberia for life.

"Don't worry," I said. "We will wake up at 6 a.m. tomorrow and travel to Ostrava. We will see what benefits you can receive. Perhaps they can find you housing."

I did not tell her that free housing was next to impossible to find in the Czech Republic. Why fuel her panic? I was beginning to understand that I had strong nerves in comparison to many of my fellow refugees. That's not to say that I did not experience anxiety, depression, and panic attacks. However, some adult refugees behaved like children all of the time, panicking to the point of impossibility. They simply could not pull themselves together and make decisions soberly. Many expected that everything would be decided for them. I forced myself not to slip into that helpless state of mind. After one week in the hostel, I pulled myself up by the bootstraps while others remained at a loss, constantly whining about how they wanted to go home, complaining life was cruel because they no longer had choices. For me, the key to survival involved being grateful to be alive and falling back on a predictable daily routine.

Seeing this woman's situation, I knew I would have to hurry up and decide where to go next, as the Czech Republic's social system was clearly on life support. I originally wanted to go to Belgium. I contacted a former coworker who had fled Ukraine and moved to Germany. She told me it was very difficult to learn the German language and get used to the German way of life. She also said that finding a job rather than working long hours as a low-paid cleaner was problematic.

My sister's American friend, Laura, said she and her husband had friends in the Netherlands who would take me in for a few nights and drop me off at a refugee center in the city of Utrecht. I liked the idea, reasoning that the Netherlands probably had more to offer than the Czech Republic. I decided to pursue that path since Laura's friends could assist me with the initial paperwork, and I would not have to burden them after that.

Still, I had concerns something could go dreadfully awry. I had read that many hostels in the Netherlands did not allow dogs. The hostels that did allow dogs were in remote places with no public transportation and little employment. Would I renounce my temporary Czech visa only to wind up in a place worse than the musty attic in Malá Morava?

"If you have any misgivings about the Netherlands, come live with us in Connecticut," Laura had written to me. "We have a big house in the country. You will have your bedroom. You can come and go as you please."

"I don't have a car and my driver's license has expired," I said.

"You can take the Connecticut driver's test in Russian," Laura explained. "You can drive our extra car as you save up for your car."

"What about Yola?" I fretted.

"Yola will come too, of course!" she replied cheerfully. "We have two dogs and a fenced-in yard. They are pack animals. They are used to living with other dogs. Yes, it will be stressful at first, but everything will settle into a routine within a few days."

"But how will I find a job?"

"This is a great time for you to find a job in America. Yes, inflation is high. It's high all over the world. But the unemployment rate in America is at record lows. You can easily find a job working with dogs, children, or the elderly. Besides, what you need to focus on now is healing. There will be no rush for you to find work. Learn the language, walk in nature, rest, heal...."

As perfect as Laura's proposal sounded, I felt like I would be imposing on her hospitality. Laura repeatedly told me that serving as my American sponsors was something she and her husband wanted to do. The problem was, I didn't want to be a mooch. The Ukrainian self-sufficiency that my parents had instilled in me was a hard thing to shake. I cringed at the thought of relying on strangers once again. Also, I had been without work for months, and the last thing I needed was more rest. I was eager to get back to living an independent, purposeful life, and earning my keep. I told Laura that I would go to the Netherlands, and if things did not work out, I would go to her.

"Okay," she answered. "But it may be harder for you to get to America once you are in the Netherlands. Your money will run out, and countries don't want refugees skirting from country to country and clogging the system with visa requests. Wherever you decide to go should be the final destination."

I was overwhelmed. "Let me think about it." Until then, I had only entertained thoughts of settling in Europe. "My Czech visa expires in six months," I wrote. "I will let you know soon."

That night, I studied English using the Duolingo app, with burgeoning thoughts of crossing the Atlantic and settling in America renewing my sense of hope. It helped that my friend who had moved to Germany decided to relocate her family to Canada. She assured me that Canada and America offered opportunities to non-English-speaking Ukrainian refugees that were not as readily available in cities throughout Europe.

I was a little anxious about learning to drive all over again and taking the driver's test in Connecticut. My Ukrainian driver's training was a joke. The private driving school offered students a rusted Fret 7 jalopy with a manual gearbox to practice on. Everything constantly broke down in that sorry excuse for a car. I recall one lesson in which I drove through a heavy downpour. The wipers stopped working and I couldn't see anything in front of me. "What should I do?" I asked the instructor. "I can't go further. Can I stop somewhere on the side of the road?"

The instructor told me to keep driving. It's a good thing that we didn't get in an accident. I couldn't reach the pedals with my feet. The seat regulator was broken, and the seat moved back and forth like a child's bouncy horse. One evening, I hurried from work to attend a driving class. The instructor was a no-show. I phoned him and asked where he was. He told me that he was too drunk to take me driving. On another occasion, the instructor had me drive on a busy roadway in the center of the city. He suddenly turned to me and said, "Sorry, I forgot that you are a new student. I didn't mean to take you here." It was truly the worst driving school in the universe.

I eventually gave up the desire to drive. Most Europeans drive cars that are much cheaper than ours in Ukraine. For example, Poland has a large used car market. However, it was expensive to have the car pass clearance at customs. In the end, I couldn't be bothered with driving a car when public transportation was readily available in Mariupol. Now it seemed I would have to change my mindset.

My dwindling interest in moving to the Netherlands was extinguished when I saw the current trend in the country involving moving Ukrainian refugees into empty prisons. The facilities were upgraded, brightly painted, and clean, but bars remained on the windows and doors, and crowds of people were everywhere. I couldn't see myself living happily in such a facility given my high levels of anxiety.

In contrast, Laura described a bucolic life in Connecticut, even stating that she and her husband planned to build a separate two-car garage with an apartment on top where I could live rent-free once the project was complete. It seemed too good to be true, but my sister assured me that Laura and her husband were the real deal. I finally set my sights on moving to America, the land of the free, home of the brave.

Laura reminded me that America was far from paradise. "It's a total mess over here right now," she wrote. "So much division, so much hate—you see it on TV and social media, but in day-to-day life, people are quite friendly. There's a strange disconnect going on, with extremists taking over the airwaves when what most people want is to live peaceful and tolerant lives. I don't understand it. Rest assured, most Americans support Ukraine, regardless of political affiliation."

Division and hate. Yes, coming from Ukraine, these were words that I understood—but if most Americans supported Ukraine, then I was willing to take the chance and go to Connecticut.

Chapter Thirty

In late July, everyone at the hostel was talking about an online video of a Ukrainian prisoner of war being tortured and castrated by a Russian soldier wearing surgical gloves and wielding a knife. The Russian stuffed the severed testicles into the POW's mouth, shot him in the head, and dragged him through the street on a rope.

For the next two days, I dropped out of life and was unwilling to do anything at all. Every time I thought of that prisoner, I would shake with rage and vengefully long for the same thing to happen to all Russian soldiers. I tried to distract myself by watching other news. Oddly, images of wildfires, droughts, and floods sweeping across every continent were easier for me to process than the news that evil spirits exist in human form and walk amongst us, regardless of how civilized the society.

One morning, a Czech volunteer asked if I was interested in giving an interview to a local television reporter about what had happened in Mariupol. I declined the invitation. It is far easier for me to write about the horrific experiences than to verbally discuss them, especially with a stranger. When I first arrived in the Czech Republic and was asked about what I experienced in Mariupol, I grew short of breath and choked back tears. I literally could not connect my words. My hope in sharing this story through the written word is to get it all out of my system and gradually let go of the memories.

I was also reluctant to expose myself to online attacks following the interview. With inflation and the cost of fuel rising across the globe, the fickle mood of some Europeans was now to support Russia. I previously made the mistake of engaging in a thread on social media in which Czechs and Italians alike told Ukrainians to give up territory in order to save future lives in Ukraine.

"Ukraine should surrender," an Italian man stated brazenly. "Only water puts out fire."

I was enraged. "It sounds like you want us to close our eyes to the crime and hand everything over to the criminal," I replied.

In typical social media fashion, the man ignored my inquiry and skipped to another subject. "Zelensky is an American puppet," he wrote. "How did you expect Russia to act when your president wanted to join NATO? Zelensky has delusions of grandeur!"

I wanted to kick this man in his virtual balls. My fingers typed furiously. "How should a man, whose country is practically unarmed and threatened by war for eight years, respond but to seek to join NATO? Now the war rages and Putin has taken vast territories of land that don't belong to him. Putin has brought great disorder to those occupied territories. Who has megalomania?"

"None of it matters in the end," the man stated. "One president cannot decide everything. There are higher minds that influence our world order—the Masons, for example."

I nearly spit out the tea I was drinking. So now a worldwide secret society was in charge? "Okay," I wrote. "If a Russian bomb comes home to you, and your loved ones die, we'll see how the decisions of higher minds like the Masons will help you."

I threw down my phone and vowed to stop engaging in frustrating social media threads about the war again. There were too many crazy people talking about things that they did not understand. For all I knew, I was arguing with a Russian bot. The internet was full of them.

It's an easy compare/contrast of the social-media experience with the real-life conversations I frequently have with friends still living in Ukraine—some of them soldiers willing to sacrifice their lives or risk being captured and tortured; others volunteering on humanitarian frontlines.

I told a female soldier friend, "If you cannot resist capture and death in battle, promise me that you will save your life and retreat."

She laughed in response. "Adoriana, we are here to the last!"

Other friends voiced the same sentiment. Ukrainians have the character of steel. Mess with us and we will show our strength. As NATO sends more sophisticated weaponry to Ukraine, I see that our cunning and intelligent warriors have learned better tactics than the Russians.

I remember the vast amount of military equipment that Russia brought into Mariupol. I don't know much about the types of weapons, but I do recall how I could hear the deafening speed of incoming shells, as though thousands flew out in an instant. The entire building would shake, along with the earth beneath our feet. We shouted to one another, "Are we going to die? How strong is this building?"

An elderly man, well-versed in the city's architecture, reassured us that the building was strong because it was recently built. The slabs were solid, he said, and the foundation possessed elements to keep it intact. His words calmed everyone.

Although our arsenal was and is outnumbered, nothing can diminish the unity and determination of our troops. I admire everything that they do. These are real Ukrainians, the present and future of our country. I sometimes wonder, *what is the secret to their courage?* It boils down to a few simple things: love for their country, love for their Ukrainian family and friends, and knowing they are defending their own land.

In comparison, the Russians have the essence of thieves. They rob and loot and expect to create a better world by washing and painting over the ruins. For this reason, many Russians choose to drink their last penny as if to say, *carpe diem, for tomorrow, is bleak.*

By early August, my parents had ceased communication. When I tried to phone or text them, there was no connection. I learned that heavy fighting and shelling were taking place in a village located ten kilometers from my parents' home. My parents don't have a basement—no one in their village has a basement. I think about them all of the time—a Russian groom and a Ukrainian bride who always lived in harmony and put the needs of one another before their own.

In mid-August, eleven refugees arrived from the Zaporizhzhia region. They told me about the intense fighting taking place in the surrounding villages. Russia had incurred heavy losses, and the Russian soldiers who survived were furious. Ukrainian prisoners of war were routinely placed in cages in front of residents in the streets and ultimately executed or lynched.

The following morning, I awoke from a dream in which I was hiding in the basement shelter as the auto parts store burned above me. Russian military stormed into the shelter and randomly fired their guns. Shells poured down from the night sky above and crumbled to the floor. I heard someone running to the floor above me.

Half dreaming, I opened my eyes and wondered how people could be running above me if I was in the attic with only a steeply pitched roof separating me from the sky. Clarity slowly kicked in. I was safely stowed away in Malá Morava, thousands of miles away from the fighting.

My phone pinged. I looked at the screen to discover a one-line text from my parents: ADORIANA, WE ARE ALIVE. I fell back to the pillow and breathed a great sigh of relief.

Chapter Thirty-One

"Oh, dear Hazel," Aphrodite folded her fan. "Such
optimism, yet you have heartrending days ahead
of you. Of course, war is coming. Love and war
always go together. They are the peaks of human
emotion! Evil and good, beauty and ugliness."
—Rick Riordan, *The Mark of Athena*

Just as families fell apart during the war, new families were
created. Ukrainians became much more decisive in their
actions because the future was too unpredictable. Many
chose to take advantage of Ukraine's wartime martial laws
that now included a provision allowing Ukrainians—both
soldiers and civilians—to apply and marry on the same day.
Before the war, a one-month wait was the norm.

There seemed to be an equal number of divorces, as
well. War is a great test of the strength of relationships.
Women married to Ukrainian soldiers either went abroad or
stayed in the country alone and worried about the safety of
their husbands. A typical Ukrainian woman experiences the
daily stress of not knowing whether her husband will live
or die. She doesn't know when—or if—she will see him
again. She doesn't know if her husband is being faithful to
her. In turn, Ukrainian fighters face a lot of temptation. The
men are considered heroes in the eyes of other women, and
ladies quite literally hang on guys, married or single, if they
wear a military uniform.

Temptations also abound for married Ukrainian women who leave the country. Many foreigners stereotype young Ukrainian women as the most beautiful in the world. They envelop the Ukrainian woman traveling abroad with so much attention and affection that she soon forgets about her man when, in fact, he needs her loyalty more than ever.

Cupid's arrow does not only strike the hearts of the younger generation. I know a fifty-five-year-old woman who lived with a man for many years in Mariupol. She took up arms right before the war began and moved to another city, where she met a man in the service. They married a few weeks later. Now they defend Ukraine together. The woman's former partner somehow survived the invasion and now lives in another city. The war threw their lives upside down but if you were to ask this woman if she is happy, she would say yes; in a different and very meaningful way, she has a *purpose.*

I remember feeling a bit envious when I saw the couple falling in love in the field outside Berdyansk. In those days, I wanted somebody to walk with, to hug and reassure me. Stepan and Artem entered my world at the perfect time. They were like brothers to me. Our manner of communication was as if I were a man. By the time I arrived in the Czech Republic, my desire to meet someone had completely disappeared. I now have other goals to focus on. However, if you ask me if there is love in a time of war, I can say with confidence—of course!

***

Thanks to the American program Uniting for Ukraine, Laura and her husband were quickly approved as my American sponsors. I submitted the required documents to the United States Citizenship and Immigration Services and was approved for travel to America and a temporary visa in a matter of weeks. Getting Yola's approval to travel overseas proved a little more difficult, but I managed to satisfy all of the requirements the CDC has for the importation of a dog that once resided in a "high-risk" country, meaning a country that did not require a rabies vaccination. Laura booked me and Yola on a direct flight from Warsaw, Poland, to JFK Airport in New York City, set to depart on September 7, 2022.

I closed my temporary Czech visa in late August and experienced a wave of tremendous relief. I had conquered a new peak in my journey. The prolonged period of stagnation was officially over. Soon I would be doing ordinary activities appropriate to a woman of my age, not twiddling my thumbs in a far-off forest. Now I was a tourist, not a refugee, since once a visa is closed in the Czech Republic, one is allowed to stay for only ninety days.

What a surreal feeling, to leave Mariupol without any personal possessions except for the clothes on my back and a cell phone, and travel to countries where everyone is a stranger at first. It reminds me of reality TV shows, where people are sent to remote islands to figure out how to survive. The final third of my life resembles that type of show. In the early months of the war, this development was extremely difficult for me to accept. Over time, I gradually embraced my circumstances and turned lemons into lemonade, convincing myself that, though difficult, at least my life is not boring.

I said a tearful goodbye to the many friends I had made in the Czech Republic. Lucas is a holy man, performing deeds of service without any expectation of payback. He apologized for not being able to find a very large travel crate for Yola per the requirements of LOT Airlines. I had previously traveled to four cities in the Czech Republic in search of a proper-sized crate without success. I reassured Lucas I would find one in Warsaw, simultaneously wondering what I would do if none were available.

"If you ever visit the Czech Republic," Lucas told me, "know that my home is always open to you and your friends." He then embraced me with all of the affection and warmth of a kind-hearted brother. As a thank-you gift, I gave him a big jar of raspberry jam made from wild raspberries I had gathered in the woodland edges and fields of Malá Morava.

My excitement intensified as my trip to America approached. I wrote to Laura, "I love this life with all of its ups and downs! My angel Yola and I are ready for new adventures! I will not leave America until I have visited every one of the major cities! Are you ready to accept these nomads?"

On my last evening in Malá Morava, I packed my bags and took one last walk in the forest with Yola. I awoke early the next morning and left the hostel without looking back.

After several bus transfers, we arrived in Ostrava, where a train would take us to Warsaw. When I arrived at the train station, I could not know from which platform my train would depart. The digital board listing train numbers and platforms was broken. I showed my ticket to a train conductor and was told the platforms were announced ten minutes before the trains arrived, which only added to my stress. As my train approached, Yola and I jumped like deer across several platforms and squeezed into the train compartment at the last second.

I had intended to use public transportation when we arrived in Warsaw. After walking a few meters, the cheap rolling luggage I had purchased in the Czech Republic fell to pieces, every wheel flying in a different direction. I was forced to call a taxi even though I spoke only a little Polish. I was so relieved when a taxi driver who spoke Russian took the call.

It took forever for the taxi to arrive due to a traffic jam. I was accustomed to the cooler weather in the mountains of the Czech Republic and so wore heavier clothing. Now I stood beneath a scorching summer sun, my sweatshirt and pants drenched in perspiration. The taxi finally arrived. The driver told me that he was from Belarus. Although Belarus is considered a close ally of Russia, the man said at least eighty percent of Belarusians supported Ukraine, but people were afraid to express their support in public.

As we drove through the congested streets of Warsaw, I was struck by how different it was from cities in the Czech Republic. Warsaw has a gray and rigid ambiance lacking any special flavor. Nevertheless, the men like to wear nicely tailored suits, and the women wear brightly colored dresses and shoes with heels. In the Czech Republic, almost everyone walks around in tracksuits and sneakers. I was also surrounded by different languages: Greek, Georgian, Ukrainian, and more.

I saw a lot of Ukrainian flags and symbols in support of Ukraine. The Poles are truly wonderful people. Many times, strangers approached to assist me if they saw I was looking for something. Ultimately, I don't think one country is better than any other country. Every nation is unique, and we all have something to learn from each other.

The taxi driver asked me about the dangerous conditions in Ukraine. I told him that both Ukrainian and Russian soldiers leave a million traps for each other—long stretches of hidden grenades and landmines. It is not uncommon for Russian soldiers to rig machine guns with transparent lines to set off a grenade when a Ukrainian soldier picks up the gun lying on the ground.

The driver dropped me off at the White House Hotel located in the Ursynów district of Warsaw. The White House is a clean and friendly establishment with gardens, and balconies offering terrific city views, and the Frederic Chopin Monument and Łazienki Royal Park are located nearby. As a Ukrainian refugee, I received a deeply discounted hotel rate.

In the two days that followed, I ran around the city trying to find a travel crate for Yola. My anxiety escalated as every pet store I entered had only small crates. At last, I found a store with one dusty large crate on the shelf. It was equally difficult for me to purchase a piece of new spinner luggage. The prices in Poland were as high as those in Ukraine, but I finally located luggage within my meager budget.

I felt a sense of accomplishment as I crawled into bed on my final night in Warsaw. *My life is finally moving forward*, I thought. *I hope it's for the better.*

Chapter Thirty-Two

My mind was a jumble of thoughts and worries during the flight to New York City. America is very expensive. How would I afford to live there independently? My sister had financially struggled in America, although she reassured me that the standard of living was much higher than in Ukraine.

When I lived in the Czech Republic, I was geographically closer to my parents and that mentally calmed me. Now I worried that I was leaving them behind to fend for themselves in Russian-occupied territory currently under heavy attack. I recalled a family with an older mother in the underground shelter in Mariupol. The old woman told her daughter to leave the shelter with her husband and child while she remained underground. The daughter tearfully begged her mother to join them. The old woman refused. The family ended up leaving the shelter without the mother. It was a heart-wrenching decision. If she later found out that her mother was killed, could she ever forgive herself for leaving her behind? Likewise, if something terrible happened to my parents, how would I forgive myself for abandoning them in Ukraine?

As I stared out the window at the passing clouds, I rebuked myself for being selfish. Why couldn't I have been courageous enough to take up arms and fight for the country I loved? I simultaneously fretted about Yola in the cargo hold. The veterinarian didn't recommend a sedative for her since she had never taken one before and he had no way of knowing how she would react. Yola is as sensitive to sharp noises as I am, and now she was in the loudest part of the plane.

I distracted myself by watching the movie *American Sniper*, which LOT Airlines offered in numerous languages. It's a good movie, although watching Bradley Cooper speak in Russian was an odd experience. When the plane landed at JFK, Ukrainian passengers were instructed to stand in a separate queue since the process of going through customs would take a long time. We were all gathered into a room and asked simple questions regarding our place of origin and our purpose in coming to America. I was exhausted because of the time difference and also stressed about Yola. She heard me answer a question and say her name, and began to yelp and whine from the next room.

"Can I see her?" I asked the customs officer.

He shook his head while rifling through my documents. "No, you can't. Sit down, please."

After three hours, all of the other Ukrainians had passed through customs and left the room, but I remained, listening to Yola whimper and howl. The inspector glanced at Yola's passport.

"Is this your dog?" he asked.

"Who else's dog would it be?" I snapped. "Is it your dog?"

He raised his voice. "I ask the questions, and you answer them. I'm just doing my job." He abruptly left his desk with my documents in hand and told me he needed to go check on something. Being sarcastic with the man was a stupid thing for me to do, I admit. However, after the long day of travel followed by a three-hour wait at US customs, my patience had run out.

A different customs officer returned with Yola in the carrier. I wanted to open the door and let her out. She had not drunk any water since boarding in Warsaw. The customs official forbade me to open the door of the carrier. I was furious but pressed my feelings down. He gave Yola water and the inspector returned. His face no longer had a menacing look; now, he even smiled as he handed me my documents. "Welcome to America," he said.

I thanked him and rushed with Yola to the sidewalk outside. My sponsors were waiting for me in a different location. I caught a Wi-Fi signal and told them where I was standing with Yola. Seconds later, Laura and her husband stood before me.

"Adoriana!" Laura said, opening her arms to embrace me.

I jerked away and broke down sobbing. I inwardly scolded myself. *Keep yourself in control. Please. Don't lose it in front of these people!* But the emotions I felt were overwhelming.

"Relax, Adoriana," she said, lightly touching my shoulder with her hand. "Now you are safe. We'll take you home."

Long lines of yellow taxis passed us on the roadway leading out of JFK. Laura pointed to the sprawling metropolis in the near distance. "That's New York City," she said, speaking into her phone translator. "I'll take you next weekend."

The images flew past the car window like frames in a movie, as if this was not happening to me but to someone else. The houses were just like those in my favorite TV series, *Desperate Housewives*—large, quaint, and brightly colored, with meticulous landscaping. The trucks and SUVs were enormous, also like the vehicles in *Desperate Housewives*. Two hours later, we arrived in the wooded hills of northwest Connecticut.

Laura provided me with a soft landing—the calm that follows the storm. My parents brought me up strictly and told me not to trust strangers. That's not to say they denied the existence of good people, but they believed one must never hope that strangers will come to one's rescue. Though I remain wary of strangers, I now see that many people wish to help with no ulterior motives. When I entered Laura's home, I sensed a positive family atmosphere. She led me and Yola upstairs to the guest room. "This is where you will sleep," she said.

The shelves held American books with Russian translations such as *The Power of Now* by Eckhart Tolle, and *The Power of Intention* by Wayne Dyer. Laura has a bright heart. She considered all of the details that would make me happy: framed photos of Yola, a dog dish for her water, and a welcoming bouquet of sunflowers on the rolltop desk. She had also purchased me a basic wardrobe comprising soft sweaters, t-shirts, leggings, casual pants, hiking boots, and sneakers, along with several types of coats.

Utterly exhausted, I immediately fell to sleep. I awoke at 2:30 a.m. and wondered if it was all a dream. I wandered like a ghoul through the downstairs rooms of Laura's house while she and her husband slept peacefully upstairs. *Welcome to the* Twilight Zone, I thought.

The next morning, Laura took me and Yola to the supermarket. I was surprised and very pleased that American grocery stores allowed dogs inside. The cashier and some of the customers smiled at Yola and did not seem the least bit concerned about her being there. I later said to Laura, "I can't believe that I was allowed inside the store with a dog! It felt strange—like I was doing something illegal."

Laura shot me a sly smile. "That's because you *were* doing something illegal," she said. "I didn't want Yola to roast in the hot car, so I decided to break the law."

That's when I realized Laura is not the innocent angel I assumed her to be. She is an angel with tiny devil's horns tucked behind her ears.

Chapter Thirty-Three

Every morning, Laura and I took Yola and Laura's two dogs for long walks along wooded trails bordering the Farmington River and a nearby lake. Yola was on cloud nine. On one walk, I met one of Laura's Ukrainian American neighbors. Evidently, Laura told the man, in English, that I was hoping to save up money to purchase a modest car so I could drive to work when my work visa is approved. They continued to converse in words I did not understand. The man and I briefly conversed in Ukrainian, and we parted ways.

As Laura led me in the direction of the parking lot, she spoke into her phone translator. "Now I have a special surprise for you," she said. "Do you see that silver Passat car over there? It belongs to the man we just met. He wants you to have it, free of charge."

I thought she was joking, I really did. "Stop it now. You're crazy."

"I mean it," she said. "It belonged to his Ukrainian father who recently passed away. He wants you to have it. He says he does not need it."

I lost all self-control and knelt on the gravel, weeping and shaking. I couldn't lift my body; my legs were like rubber. I looked up at Laura. "Why would he do that?" I asked in shock.

Laura shrugged casually. "Why wouldn't he?"

As the saying goes, some people are a lesson to us, others are a blessing. In America, I met so many people who were not indifferent to my fate. They offered support, both verbally and financially. For example, the local Lions Club mailed me a check for five hundred dollars without ever meeting me in person. This money will be applied to car repairs and insurance.

It took me hours to recover from the Ukrainian American man's act of kindness. I had experienced so much ugliness and hate in the past months, not to mention the deaths of innocent people, innocent animals, and a beautiful and peaceful country battered and broken by shells. This man came along and spoke to me with such gentleness and concern. He broke all the stereotypes I had previously harbored. He gave me faith in the victory of good over evil. The victory of Ukraine.

A similar spontaneous act of generosity happened when Laura and I went to New York City the following weekend. After gorging on authentic Italian pizza and red wine in Little Italy, we walked past an Eastern European church donning blue and yellow ribbons, sunflowers, and the Ukrainian flag. A large sign above the church doorway read Pray For Ukraine. As I took photos of the church, a man drove up in a minivan and asked where we were from. He was a Romanian priest wearing layman's clothing, and he also spoke Ukrainian. I introduced myself and we conversed. As we said goodbye, he handed me a crisp American dollar bill. I refused to take it, but Laura snatched it away from him and forced it into my hand. I looked down, expecting to see five dollars or even ten dollars. The man had given me one hundred dollars. Again, I wept like a fool. I could not comprehend such generosity.

When we boarded the train from Bridgeport, Connecticut, to Grand Central Station the day before, Laura pulled out a zip-lock bag containing cherries and grapes. "Want some?" she asked.

I laughed. "You are like the grannies in Ukraine who always travel with food. They bring hardboiled eggs and baked chickens in their luggage. As soon as the train sets in motion, the trays come down and the old Ukrainians start to crack off the eggshells, stinking up the car." I told her how the older generation in Ukraine has such character. They boisterously laugh and shout and get into squabbles on the trains. They are like wild little children living in an earlier and less sophisticated era.

We ate lunch at a casual American franchise, Just Salad, located near the hotel. I asked Laura what the orange cubes in my chicken and kale salad were called. "Sweet potatoes," she answered. "Don't you eat them in Ukraine?"

"I've never seen a sweet potato in my life," I said. "Yes, they are quite good."

As we walked the streets of Upper and Lower Manhattan. I was struck by the sheer strength, intelligence, and power of mankind. To design and build such huge and gorgeous buildings with human hands, to draw people from all nations, to foster the arts with such zest. The sounds of street music, the mouthwatering scents of freshly baked pretzels and souvlaki emanating from food carts, the unbelievable and crazy rhythm of a city that never sleeps. *Why would anyone choose war over this?* I thought.

We visited many of the traditional tourist sites. I met two Ukrainian women on the ferry ride around the Statue of Liberty. We warmly chatted as Neil Diamond sang "Coming to America," followed by Sinatra's timeless rendition of "New York, New York." Yes, it was schmaltzy but incredibly fun. Lady Liberty is also much smaller than I imagined. Don't get me wrong, I am well aware of America's checkered history regarding its treatment of immigrants, past and present, but I was willing to put that reality aside if only for one day and embrace the fairy tale.

Times Square surpassed my wildest expectations. So much shameless capitalism on display! I loved it and recognized many of the stores and brands that we also have in Ukraine, albeit at much higher costs. Looking at the enormous, brightly colored digital billboards in such high definition almost made me dizzy. One depicted a giant three-dimensional alien creature poking his head out of the canvas and reaching his arm into the street as if to touch pedestrians walking past.

The tour of the Empire State Building was surprisingly entertaining. There were photos of many celebrities who visited the landmark in the past, including King Kong and Mr. Bean. An observation deck on the eighty-sixth floor offered a full, stunning three-hundred-and-sixty-degree view of Midtown on a gloriously warm and sunny September afternoon. I tried to push the thought from my head that the beautiful city stretched out below me could one day turn to dust, like Mariupol.

We returned to Connecticut to find Yola in her favorite spot, on the second-floor outdoor deck, looking down at a family of deer. They cross the backyard every evening to eat apples that have fallen down onto the grass. She has a special affection for a buck with elegant antlers who stops by every night to stare back at her with an equally fixed fascination. Like Yola, I too was beginning to relax. In Connecticut, the anxiety that plagued me in Ukraine and even in the Czech Republic lessened by the day, replaced by positive emotions and experiences.

I recently went to the immersive Van Gogh art exhibit in Hartford. My mother would have loved it. I plunged into the multi-dimensional masterpieces flowing across the walls and floors and felt like I was looking into a soul that radiated beauty. Van Gogh's father wanted him to be a preacher, but he chose to pursue painting instead. He made little profit from his artwork in his lifetime and fought against society's pressure to conform. Still, he remained true to his quest for beauty, and today we see how the gift in his works continues to instill inspiration and hope in the hearts of people all over the world.

A wall display posted an excerpt from a letter that Van Gogh wrote to his brother Theo in 1882. Van Gogh's words connected with me in a way that they would never have before the war began.

> I also believe that it may happen that one succeeds, and one mustn't begin by despairing; even if one loses here and there, and even if one feels a sort of decline, the point is nevertheless to revive and have courage, even though things don't turn out as one first thought.

My life has not even remotely turned out as I first thought. Before the war, I lived in a cocoon. I had a daily routine in Mariupol, and I thought very little about world events. Everything changed for Ukrainians when the war began. We suddenly understood that trouble can come to your doorstep when you least expect it, and a nation must unite with other democracies to fight against evil.

I have heard it said that one man started this war, and only one man can end it. However, as I write these closing words in late September 2022, I wonder if the Russian *people* can end this horrible war. Can they overcome Putin's maniacal schemes through protests and the refusal to give their lives for his greedy ambitions? And what will happen when a shark like Putin is cornered? Will he resort to tactical nuclear warfare? How far will this madman go?

The story of my escape from Mariupol and my life as a refugee is a mere grain of sand on a beach containing millions of grains; each one tells the story of an individual Ukrainian's suffering and sorrow since the first shells dropped over Mariupol on February 24, 2022. Thanks to love, this world continues to exist. May we always love and strive for peace on Earth. Thank you for taking the time to read my story, dear reader.

Glory to the heroes, and glory to Ukraine!

For More News About Adoriana Marik and Anne K. Howard, Signup For Our Newsletter:

http://wbp.bz/newsletter

Word-of-mouth is critical to an author's long-term success. If you appreciated this book please leave a review on the Amazon sales page:

http://wbp.bz/mariupol

**AVAILABLE FROM ANNE K. HOWARD
AND WILDBLUE PRESS!**

HIS GARDEN by ANNE K. HOWARD

http://wbp.bz/hisgardena

A lawyer gets inside the mind of a notorious New England serial killer in this award-winning and "grimly compelling" true crime (Kirkus).

**AVAILABLE FROM DEBORAH VADAS
LEVISON AND WILDBLUE PRESS!**

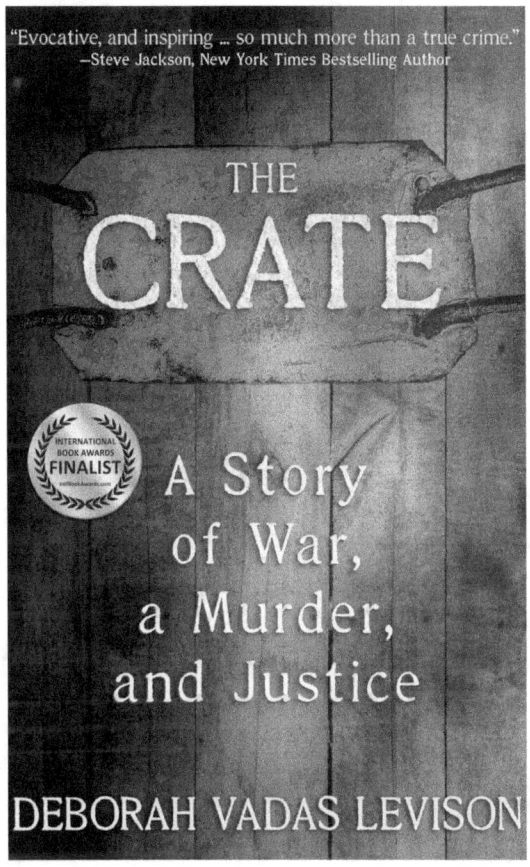

THE CRATE by DEBORAH VADAS LEVISON

http://wbp.bz/cratea

The multiple award-winning account of Holocaust
survival and present-day murder. *"Evocative, and
inspiring . . . So much more than a true crime."*
—Steve Jackson, New York Times bestselling author

**AVAILABLE FROM ROBERT DODGE
AND WILDBLUE PRESS!**

TEMPEST-TOST by ROBERT DODGE

http://wbp.bz/tta

*"Dodge takes us behind the headlines and introduces
real people and their very real struggles yearning
to breathe free. Page-turning [and] proactive."* —
Craig McGuire, author of *Brooklyn's Most Wanted*

**AVAILABLE FROM MARGARITA
NELIPA AND WILDBLUE PRESS!**

KILLING RASPUTIN by MARGARITA NELIPA

http://wbp.bz/killingrasputina

*A look into the life of the so-called "Mad Monk"
of Imperial Russia, his murder, and the effects of
his death on a dynasty, a people, and a country.*

www.ingramcontent.com/pod-product-compliance
Lightning Source LLC
Chambersburg PA
CBHW061151120626
46546CB00005B/2015